O's

Little Guide
to the Big
Questions

Other Titles in O's Little Books Series

O's Little Book of Happiness
O's Little Guide to Finding Your True Purpose
O's Little Book of Love & Friendship
O's Little Guide to Starting Over
O's Little Book of Calm & Comfort

O's

Little Guide
to the Big
Questions

The Editors of *O, The Oprah Magazine*

FLATIRON
BOOKS
NEW YORK

The Library of Congress Cataloging-in-Publication Data is available upon request.

ISBN 978-1-250-07012-8 (hardcover)
ISBN 978-1-250-07013-5 (ebook)

Our books may be purchased in bulk for promotional, educational, or business
use. Please contact your local bookseller or the Macmillan Corporate and
Premium Sales Department at 1-800-221-7945, extension 5442, or by email
at MacmillanSpecialMarkets@macmillan.com.

First Edition: January 2018

10 9 8 7 6 5 4 3 2 1

I've always thought of myself as a seeker. . . . I am beguiled by the mystery of life.

—OPRAH WINFREY

Contents

How Do I Live a Full Life?

An Education, *Amy Maclin*   3

Facing Down Fear, *Michelle Wildgen*   15

Small House, Big World, *David McGlynn*   19

Walk Away, *Elissa Schappell*   23

Slipping Past Borders, *Katherine Russell Rich*   25

What About Love?

Double Jeopardy, *Rita Wilson*   35

Strings Attached, *April Wilder*   45

Divorce Dreams, *Ellen Tien*   57

The Halfway House, *Jessica Ciencin Henriquez*   67

Meant to Be, *Julie Orringer*   71

CAN I HANDLE THE HARD TIMES?

Feel Your Feelings, *Katie Arnold-Ratliff* 77

Not to Look Away, *Marie Howe* 81

You Can See, *Thich Nhat Hanh* 85

My Mother's Daughter, *Bonnie Jo Campbell* 87

Come What May, *Joan Silber* 91

WHAT REALLY MATTERS?

Yes and No, *Valerie Monroe* 95

Finders, Keepers, Hoarders, Weepers, *Michelle Herman* 97

Give Yourself a Happiness Raise, *Margarita Bertsos* 111

Sweet Charity, *Catherine Newman* 115

Helpfulness, *Gloria Steinem* 119

Thanks for the Memories, *Alice McDermott* 123

WHAT DOES IT ALL MEAN?

Vision, *Kate Braestrup* 129

My Mother's Journals, *Terry Tempest Williams* 133

Blinded by the Light, *Martha Beck* 141

Cooper's Heart, *Rebecca Gummere* 151

The Point, *Barbara Ehrenreich* 173

Contributors 177

How Do I Live a Full Life?

Pay attention.
Be astonished.
Tell about it.

—MARY OLIVER

An Education

Amy Maclin

———◦❧◦———

For seventeen years, I spent most of my waking hours in school doodling. I learned the types of clouds and what happens to a banana when you put it in liquid nitrogen. But there were never any classes on how to live. I wanted to know what we need to do to be happy, and how to make love last, and why we should keep washing the dishes when *we're all going to die someday.*

In the absence of formal instruction, I became a self-help geek. My teenage raids on my mother's book closet taught me about erroneous zones and bad things that happened to good people and how Helen Gurley Brown was *Having It All*, which had me eagerly awaiting the prurient thrills of adulthood. (Still waiting.) After college I entered a diaphanous phase of Jungian archetypes; I greeted

the millennium with Buddhist titles about the essential-
ness of emptiness—each one beautifully executed yet un-
satisfying, like trendy foam food.

As I hurtled into my forties, I knew I was lucky—I had
a good husband, friends, interesting work—but I worried
that I didn't deserve it all, or that I was messing it up, or
that everything would be taken away. I'd been an outwardly cheerful kid who was desperate to keep everyone
happy but lay awake wondering, *What if the world ends?*
Now I was an outwardly cheerful adult who did the same.
I had the rest of my life to figure things out, but the rest
of my life didn't seem like a long time anymore. Some
things were changing rapidly (the topography of my skin,
the resilience of my knees), and some things wouldn't be
changing at all (I'd always be a sensitive tub of goo, and
I'd never be a mother—my choice, but so final). I still
hadn't grown up, and yet I was growing old.

It felt obscene to gnaw on my fears and regrets, because
I was *loved*. How could I feel adrift in a universe where I
had an embarrassment of riches? I had my husband, who
held me when I was angry or sick or both. When I wept
about the future—mine or our swiftly tilting planet's—he'd

say things that took my ungrateful breath away, like "But you'll always have me." The trouble with being forty-four years old was that I knew I might not.

No one can think about this stuff all the time and still live in the world, so I got therapy and figured I'd just grimace and bear it. But then I found out that there really is a School of Life.

Headquartered in a London storefront, the school offers courses on the essential human conundrums, such as How to Choose a Partner or How to Make Your Mind Up. Founder Alain de Botton, writer of such cheekily pop-philosophical books as *How Proust Can Change Your Life*, wanted to create a place where ordinary people could illuminate their ordinary problems with insights gathered from literature or philosophy—Tolstoy on family happiness, Thoreau on solitude. "It's tragic that everyone thinks they have to work everything out for themselves, because they don't," says de Botton. "No more than we have to work out physics for ourselves."

Since childhood I've been fascinated by stories about hidden worlds lurking behind some ordinary door, like Narnia. The School of Life seemed magical that way, tucked across the street from a place that sold Union Jack umbrellas (a number of which I bought and then forgot in pubs all over central London). Above the dark blue door, stenciled yellow letters promised GOOD IDEAS FOR EVERYDAY LIFE.

Inside, the requisite bookstore was airy and light, customers murmuring in English and Japanese, someone gently placing the lid on a china teapot. It was the way I wanted things to be in my head. I promptly bought a "Utopia Candle," inspired by Thoreau's Walden Pond, with a top note of wild berries, and a "Psychoanalytic Pencil Set," each one engraved with a psychological term (e.g., DEFENCE MECHANISM). It was a boutique of self-help, and I was grooving on it.

I couldn't pass up *How to Develop Emotional Health*, 141 pages long and pop-art pink with one upturned curve on the cover; look again and you realize it's a smile. This is the school's brand of wink-wink, nudge-nudge message: *We know that* you *know it's ridiculous to think a book that's half an inch thick could tell you everything about "how to develop emotional health." But we know you wish it could. We wish it could, too. The absurdity of it all! Together, we'll figure out what we can.*

Even the teachers embodied this roll-up-your-sleeves whimsy: Cathy, who said her creative muse had the fearlessness of Vivienne Westwood and the patience of Mr. Miyagi from *The Karate Kid*; John-Paul, who spent a year making his own clothes and wrote a book about it called *Sew Your Own*. As for the attendees, they ran the gamut: tattooed creative types, young mothers, thirty-ish guys in football jerseys, pillowy older ladies whom I hoped would call me "Ducky."

I've always been privately appalled by group therapy. All those judgmental strangers in chairs circled like one of the descending rings of hell. However, at The School of Life I found my fellow students funny and charming, prone to saying things like "People with a high degree of self-mastery and self-knowledge—I envy those bastards." In How to Stay Calm, everyone shared the triggers of their anxiety and rage, like transatlantic flights or the ex-husband who's "an absolute knob." None of it applied to me, and I wrote smugly in my notes, "No big revelations here." Then a fifty-something man with the tiniest hole in his wool sweater said with urgency, "What if your anxiety is more low-level but . . . chronic? Since I turned forty, I've been walking around with it all the time." I sat up straighter then. I knew this song by heart.

It's not that I'm constantly agonizing over the passing of time. It's more intermittent than that. I'll just be looking into a mirror with my head tilted a tiny bit and I'll see it—the skin that pulls at the hollow of my neck, so thin and delicate that I might as well be made of gauze. Then the fear slips up from behind and puts me in a choke hold. But when I look around at the bright world with its crisp edges, everyone is joking about wrinkles, each passing birthday that, *hardy-har,* "beats the alternative!" It was a balm to see another human being carrying the same burden I did, this middle-manager type who could be standing behind me in a sandwich line. I fought the urge to turn to him and shout, "ME TOO!" I didn't think I'd ever fully felt the power of those two words before.

When I caught up with him at the break, he said, "What did you do for *your* fortieth? I just went into a cave." I brightened. "Oh, a *cave*! Where?" He said, "Er, not an actual cave. I just stayed in my apartment." I asked, "It gets better, though, right?" He looked at me kindly and answered, "Somewhat."

At the beginning of each class, we were asked to write a newspaper headline about why we were there. In How to Balance Work with Life, our example was PRESSURIZED MANAGER DESPERATE FOR DATING TIME! I put pen to paper— and stopped. How could I know myself so little when I thought about me constantly? Had I been thinking, or was it just ruminating, the thing a cow does when she chews her regurgitated feelings—I mean, food?

The truth was, I had a secret shame. In all those self-help books I read, I never did the exercises. They would have just slowed me down, and I needed to move on to the next book because my self needed a lot of help. When John-Paul asked us to write about how we hid our work identities at home and our home identities at work, I felt a squirming eighth-grade restlessness and mentally willed him not to call on me. This is the downside of being in school: Someone in charge forces you to work. John-Paul reminded us that we had to make a conscious effort to find time for the things that mattered. And then he called on me. "What could you lose in order to gain?" he asked. I said, "Watch less TV?"

In college I had a sadistic English professor who had been forced to postpone her own education because she'd been busy having five children, as she frequently and bitterly reminded us. We were children ourselves, who had the luxury of learning all day, and by God, we would not squander it on her watch. She ran that class as if we were on Parris Island, making us drop and give her twenty stanzas: "SIR, YES SIR! DYLAN THOMAS, *FERN HILL*, SIR!" We hated her.

But years later, I still remember *Fern Hill*, those last lines: *Time held me green and dying / Though I sang in my chains like the sea.* Dr. Sarge gave me discipline then and sustenance forever. I had required so much of the self-help books I'd read, but I had required nothing of myself.

All these insights smelled suspiciously like epiphanies. Suspicious is how I felt about epiphanies, because my own never lasted: I'd open my heart to humanity, and then some nimrod would block the napkin dispenser at Starbucks and I'd have to close it again. What good is a redemption story if you can't stay redeemed? I put this question to Roman Krznaric, one of the school's founding faculty members.

"We do a course in mindfulness or we take a dance class, and we feel full of inspiration—but the feeling fades," he said. "The reality is that we don't 'find' meaning or direction but grow them, through the rough-and-tumble of life. There's a lovely Leonardo da Vinci line—he declared that experience was his mistress. *That's* how we learn, through experiment and change."

Experiment and change could take a long time, though, and writing a check takes a second—which may be why I once paid several hundred dollars for a class on how to breathe. When it was over, I stopped breathing in any kind of organized way, and I felt betrayed. I had shown up and *paid*. Wasn't that enough? This is what happens in a free-market economy where we have little time and less patience, Krznaric told me: Once we've thrown money at a problem, we want an on-the-spot solution, preferably with a warranty. He said lightly, "You wanted to buy your happiness."

I thought about experiments—a cornerstone of the scientific method, as I learned in high school when we shattered our cryogenically frozen banana. No one performs an experiment once and considers her work done. She repeats it with different variables, correcting what she thought she knew, incorporating what she's learned. Without tests, we'd never get to the facts. Why should it be so different with the truth?

The classes on creativity and ambition were packed, but there were only about fifteen students in How to Face Death. (They'd told me at the front desk that this one can be a hard sell.) One woman had come because her ninety-eight-year-old mother was dying of cancer and refused to acknowledge it. A slightly graying man nodded to the woman beside him and said, "It's our anniversary, and my wife thought this would be a nice way to end the week."

My own crisis of mortality had unspooled when my cat died, the year I turned forty. After the vet gave her that last shot, it was over so fast: She was there and then she wasn't, and I was left holding her blankets. She'd been with me eighteen years. Living suddenly seemed more conditional than it had before. I couldn't stand to put my ear to my husband's chest, because his heart might stop beating while I lay there listening.

In class we learned that the American education activist Parker J. Palmer once compared death to winter, which "clears the landscape." Newcomers to the Upper Midwest, he wrote, are often advised: "The winters will drive you crazy until you learn to get out into them." Walk straight ahead into winter—literal or metaphorical—or the dread of it will rule your life.

Our exercise, adapted from poet Stephen Levine's *A Year to Live*, was our walk into winter: We'd imagine that we were going to die in 365 days and plan the time we had left, month by month, conversations we'd like to have, things we'd longed to do.

I'd always assumed I'd ... travel. I'd travel to ... where? I wrote "Asia" because that covered a lot of ground. I wrote "India," and then put a question mark because it's so hot. I looked at the blank spots on the page. Filling them would have to be my homework.

Facing Down Fear

Michelle Wildgen

It's pitch-dark on this western edge of Costa Rica, and I'm in a car with my husband and our two-and-a-half-year-old daughter, creeping along an unpaved road with steep angles and blind curves, our tires grinding against an axle-snapping mixture of rock and dirt. I can sense the drop-off only inches to my right. And I'm afraid. It's suddenly clear to me that this vacation was a mistake and we should never have come here: This is the wrong country, the wrong car, and what seems to be the wrong road, because we can't find our rental house. Any minute we are going to flip over and plunge down the side of this mountain.

And then, as we reach a particularly steep spot, I see a sign for a bar.

When my husband was still drinking, he barely made it home most nights. During those hours I called his cell compulsively or waited by my phone, terrified it wouldn't ring, terrified it would. Some of what I dreaded came true—a policeman would answer the cell phone, or my caller ID would show the name of a hospital. That was a long time ago, and what calms me now in the face of my most profound fears is not reassurance that nothing bad will happen, but that some of it has, and here we still are. You do not self-destruct when your fears come to pass. Things are replenishable that you thought were not: your savings, your opportunities, your pride. Your life can be stripped very close to the bone, and you can begin again.

My husband has been sober for nearly a decade, and while I count us lucky, I know bad things can still happen— like a missed hairpin turn in the darkest part of the night. Surviving fear does not make one immune to fear. Even on my best days there are times when I think, *When you're as happy as this is when you lose it all.* Who doesn't look at her husband's neck or her daughter's curls and wonder at how the human body—these bodies, the ones you love the most—can ever be kept safe? They can't. Things befall us, things we can't imagine. But we survive. We awaken from the bad dream of crisis, rise, and keep moving. We learn to live not with a loss, as if we accept or welcome it, but alongside it.

I believe in preventing what I can, in life insurance and seat belts. But I also believe there's life to be found on the other side of fear. I believe in continuing up the mountain, petrifying though it is, until you see the lights of the rental house. I believe in getting some sleep once you arrive, so that in the morning you can see the view you could not see in the dark: the coconut trees that blanket the mountainside, the coves beyond the cliff, the mist above the shining green agate of the ocean. The peaceful place you didn't know was waiting.

Small House, Big World

David McGlynn

We'd lived in our first house since our oldest son was two and before our youngest was born. Over the years we'd refinished floors, replaced cracked tile, and strung lights across the backyard. But there was no changing the square footage, and as our sons grew, the place began to feel cramped. The four of us battled over one shower. I fell down the basement stairs carrying laundry because the steps were so crowded with shoes and jackets. Whenever my in-laws visited, we squeezed cheek by jowl into the living room. In the morning, I'd find my father-in-law's toothbrush French-kissing mine in the medicine cabinet. It was agreed: We needed a bigger home.

That February, we found one with walk-in closets, an updated kitchen, and three bathrooms, each private enough to guarantee I'd never again listen to an overnight guest move his bowels while I sipped my coffee. We made an offer. It was accepted. The terms were agreeable. All we had to do was sell our house.

For months we invited strangers to peek in our closets and cupboards. We shook hands with young couples on the cusp of childbearing, and I pointed out the other kids on the street, the long driveway where I'd taught the boys to ride a bike. More than once we heard a buyer whisper, "This could be the one."

But the offers didn't come. We lowered the price, and still no one was interested. By June, we'd paid for an inspection on the new place and visited the school the boys would attend, ignoring the fact that not a soul had shown up for our last two open houses. On July 1, we had no choice but to let our offer expire. Another family swooped in and bought the house I'd foolishly thought of as ours.

That August, we went to Ireland. A friend had offered us a month in his family's County Clare cottage, an old farmhouse on the peninsula. It was my sons' first time abroad. Six months earlier, I'd been certain our buying and selling would have concluded long before the trip. Now it felt like a retreat from our failures.

The house was even tinier than ours, a single main room and two small bedrooms. Donkeys grazed in the garden along the side windows, eyeballing us while we dressed or read, belting out guttural brays that crescendoed into full-throated hee-haws. We laughed every time we heard them, and we heard them a lot.

One windy day we boarded a ferry bound for the Aran Islands, off the western coast. The boat looked broad and sturdy in the harbor, but once it reached the open sea, the pleasure cruise became a spewfest. A family nearby bent forward in unison and vomited into the plastic barf bags the crew had handed out. A little girl clutched her father's neck and wailed, "Make it stop! Make it stop!"

I turned to check on the boys, seated behind me. Their hands were in the air, grins on their faces. And it hit me: The house I'd yearned for *wasn't* necessary. There were things in life far more enduring than a house or the stuff houses contain. Exhibit A: my sons whooping and hollering as we motored toward a stunning place they'd never seen before.

That day my wife and I decided to stay in our house and indulge our lust for the world. We wanted our boys to see adventure as a lifelong value rather than a diversion reserved for the newly graduated or the retired. Our house might be small, but our lives—with careful budgeting and a little gumption—could be big.

Since Ireland, we've walked the length of Manhattan and hiked the Rock of Gibraltar and swum in the Caribbean Sea at dusk on Christmas Eve. We've done it on the cheap, holing up in hostels. We've eaten winkles and dillisk, *morcilla* smothered in peppers, octopus grilled next to the water where it was caught. The boys, now twelve and ten, have stopped asking when we're going to move. Now they just want to know where we're going next.

Walk Away

Elissa Schappell

After my first book was published, in 2000, I spent two and a half years writing a novel. But it never felt right. I didn't even name it; it was the poor, misshapen beast child I kept hidden under my bed. When I finally showed it to my agent, she said, "None of the things you do well are in evidence here." I was devastated, then relieved: I had failed, and now I could stop. If you don't feel a shiver of excitement or fear, if there's no emotional risk involved, let it go. You can't discount how hard it will be to leave your bad marriage or stop writing your bad book, but if you're unhappy, nothing can get better as long as the status quo stays the status quo.

Slipping Past Borders

Katherine Russell Rich

In 1988 I was diagnosed with cancer and launched into an alien world—a bizarre, distorted landscape—and I didn't have a map. Where I'd come from, people defined their lives by the things they loved: their friends, their family, those nights in late summer when shooting stars are as thick as miraculous blizzards in the sky. But in this new world, definitions can be hard to come by. Here, certainty is an illusion.

Here, you live among outlaws, your body's own cells: Whole phalanxes of them turn mutinous, become silent killers. This is a country that's both narrow and vast, where geography bends at the edges and landmarks vanish like Cheshire cats. "Oh, we don't use that drug anymore," a doctor will say, five minutes after the drug was invented.

So you have to become your own cartographer, make your own way. You grow fluent in an ornate language you won't use on the other side. "Neoplasia" and "hematopoietic" are words that can startle new acquaintances, especially if, as is true with me, for the most part your treatments don't alter your appearance. If your side effects are outwardly mild, you slide across borders undetected. In my case, there was a notable exception: the stretch, fifteen years back, when I had a bone-marrow transplant and was feeble and white, a bald worm woman, ghostly.

Five years later, the doctors told me that the average life expectancy was two and a half years with stage IV breast cancer, breast being the variety I have. (Stage IV means the cancer has spread, is deadly. No turning back. No cure.) I hasten to add that two and a half years is just an average. It's not unusual for people to reach five, even ten. Get much past that, though, and they decide you fall into a small subcategory of people who inexplicably live for years: twenty, thirty, or, with all the new stuff coming down the pike, who knows? Maybe a normal life span.

Here, through the looking glass, in the back of the beyond, there is no normal. There is no certainty, but that's true in the old world as well. (This is something many people don't want to know, so I mostly keep it to myself.) Another truth that applies to both places: Uncertainty is not necessarily to be feared. It can make your life bloom, give you power; at least that's what I've found.

In the months before and after my bone-marrow transplant, I conducted an experiment: What would happen if I said exactly what I thought? Fights on planes, that's what. Gallows-humor jokes that made people blanch. ("Sure takes the term out of terminal," said of advanced but sluggish cancer, requires a special audience.) Near-ejection from art galleries. In that case I'd opened my mouth, as if possessed, and voiced what had been my private opinion of the brittle gallery owner who was aggressively dismissive when I politely asked for directions. What I said, exactly, was, "You're a bitch." She looked startled and answered slowly, "Well, maybe I am." And I felt, for the moment, elated. However clumsy and crude I was during those months, it was the beginning of learning to take on power, of discovering how to speak up. It would be a while before I got comfortable with it.

Ten years after my diagnosis, three years after my

bone-marrow transplant, at forty-two I didn't yet know that I fell into any subcategory, only that I was several years past my stated expiration date. "The way this cancer's come on so fast," the raw-boned oncologist who diagnosed me with stage IV had said, "you have a year or two to live." Years later, she'd no longer be a practicing doctor and I'd be alive and kicking, but again, I didn't know that yet.

But here are some things I was starting to know: When you're swamped by fear, ask yourself "How are you right now? Right now, are you in the hospital? Right now, are tumors swelling in your spine, cracking bones, forcing you into a fetal position?" The one time they were doing just that, I was flown to North Carolina for a procedure that, it turned out, I was too sick to begin. In a last-ditch effort, a doctor tried a hormone treatment no one had used much since the sixties, and in a turn that still seems impossible, the cancer, for no good reason, retreated and lay down, where it has pretty much remained. Every so often it snarls and raises its head, and we switch treatments. We smack it back down.

"How are you now?" I learned to ask myself whenever

I feel an ominous buzz in a bone, whenever uncertainty threatens to swamp me. "How are you right now?" And each time, the answer is "Fine. Stay right here, in this day, stay right here in your mind." That's one of the things I say to counsel myself. Also: "Leave room for the God factor; no one can say, with ultimate truth, what will happen." And: "When you're afraid to move forward, ask yourself what's the worst that can happen." One night, on chemo, I was comparing notes on the phone with a friend, another cancer patient, who said, "When you're fighting the insurance companies, don't you ever think, *What are they going to do, kill me?*" It is, I've decided, an exemplary motto.

Furthermore, this: "Keep going and don't look down; if you do, you'll hit," though this one I can't manage perfectly. I still think I'm going to die soon. I fall and hit bottom all the time.

Twelve years after my diagnosis, five years after the transplant: I quit my profession, magazine editing, and became a writer. The illness had made physical adventures harder. "Fine," I decided. "Then I'll have adventures of the mind—and, perhaps, some impact on the world." When I was told I was going to die, I was shredded to realize I hadn't made any real difference. The life of a writer was uncertain, but as a writer, it seemed, I might leave a mark.

Out of the blue one day a newspaper assignment came through, to go to India and interview the Dalai Lama's doctor. Just for two weeks, but I was terrified to travel there alone, terrified of all the ghastly bad ends that awaited me in the unknown.

But so what? "Just try it. Stay right here, in this day," I said to myself again. After all, I only had to book the ticket, not meet fourteen terrible fates.

And so I took the trip. And when I returned I took a Hindi lesson, for fun, to preserve the memory. Each class forced me into a concentration that shifted between frustration and wonder. Sentences produced vertigo. Verbs came at the end. "I this shop from some fruit buy want" could retain its meaning only if I didn't look down. I'd hold my breath and push off, like skiing.

Then a friend suggested I spend a year in India learning Hindi. "Just try it." And so I moved to the desert state of Rajasthan, to an ancient, sloping home where murals of tiger hunts ran the length of the walls. In the thin lane below, magnificent temples tucked between shops, I'd pass two tired-looking old men in a storefront, bent over the silver anklets they sold. Down the street, a cheerful boy polished bracelets in a vat of milky water. When I'd stop to watch, his father, his fingers *mehndi*'ed red, would advise *aritha,* an Indian fruit, for my hair. He brought out three small, wrinkled orbs and told me to boil them in water. "For soft and silky," he said in Hindi.

Twenty-two years after diagnosis, fifteen years after the transplant, right now. "When you were really sick, you had to test your limits," a friend had said on the eve of the second trip, after confessing she was worried I'd be found by the side of some road. "And now maybe you have to keep doing that." I was peeved at the time, thinking she was implying I was down a few marbles, but now I think there was some truth to what she said. That experience was only partly about learning Hindi; it was as much about learning not to accept limits—of cancer, of anything.

What I know now: Even if I had had a map from the start, it wouldn't have done me any good. Like old lives, maps in this world, or any world, are something of an illusion. They change all the time. Now, when fear threatens to shut me down, I think back to how, after I'd told my oncologist I wanted to go live in India, he was silent for a bit. I don't think he'd had a patient with advanced cancer ask to do anything like this. "All right," he said finally, "but you have to be closely monitored." I agreed, then got over there to find that no oncologists practiced within hundreds of miles of the town where I'd landed. We rallied, my doctor and I. He did his best to answer all my crazed late-night emails—"I feel a pain in my hip. Do you think that's from cancer or riding in rickshaws?"—and I set up a relay system, whereby vials of my blood repeatedly changed hands before ending up at a lab in Mumbai to be tested.

In other words, we made it up as we went along, something you learn to do if you stick around long enough. And here's something else you find: You may not have known it, but, really, that's all you've been doing the whole time. Along with everyone else.

What About Love?

It's more than worth it—just don't let them
tell you it's bliss.

—AMY BLOOM

Double Jeopardy

Rita Wilson

It's a sunny, Sunday California morning. My husband is driving me, my mother and father, and two of our four children to church. This is the same church where I was baptized with my brother (two for the price of one!), where my sister was married and I was her maid of honor, where my husband and I were married, and where both our youngest children were christened in the baptismal font.

Driving on the freeway, my mother, who is vibrantly curious after eighty-six years of life and fifty-six years of marriage, tells us about something she heard on the radio. She has been pondering this question, thanks to the airwaves: If you knew at twenty-five what you know today about your spouse, would you still marry the same person?

Since it is already a beautiful day, my husband and I add to its beauty by responding instantly, that, yes, we would marry each other knowing what we know now. My father, although not usually available for this sort of discussion, generously engages and answers that, yes, he would marry my mother all over again. My mother, always interested in good discussion, responds delightfully in her thick Greek accent as if she knows the question to the "Double Jeopardy!" answer: "Not me!"

Now, please understand that my parents are Greek and Bulgarian. The idea that this is a subject one would only discuss after five years of therapy never enters anyone's mind. (When you are Mediterranean, you just speak now, argue later . . . or maybe you eat now, argue later.) Certainly, these two people, who are sitting with their arms brushing against each other, are not about to announce they are splitting up. I'm pretty sure that after nearly six decades, three children, and six grandchildren, they have the marriage thing down. But I have no idea where my mom is going with this.

Before we go anywhere, though, let me start at the beginning. In 1946 my Bulgarian dad "jumped ship" in Philadelphia, then made his way to New York City, eagerly learning English while working at the St. Regis Hotel. My Greek mother had escaped from her ethnically Greek but geographically Albanian village during the war, arriving in New York via Athens with her mother, sister, and two brothers.

My parents met in 1950 in New York City, at a dance where my dad eyed my mom across a crowded room. He wooed her briefly and then asked her to marry him. My mother, still new to the United States, thought maybe she should wait a bit—sow some oats, or sew some coats, really, because that was her job at a factory. After a few dates, and no acceptance of my dad's proposal, they amicably parted ways.

A year later, they met again. A friend of my mother's saw my handsome dad across the dance floor and declared, "If you don't want him, I do. He's nice." There is nothing like someone else's recognition of a good catch to wake you up. My mom, now another year older, realized that she missed my dad. So she pushed her friend aside like a desperate contestant on *Dancing with the Stars* and box-stepped the night away.

My parents didn't have a sweep-you-off-your-feet sort of romance. They were both too practical for that. But they loved each other and saw the goodness each possessed. Soon they found themselves planning their wedding, their lives, and their future. About three weeks before the wedding, my dad had some concerns. He worried he might not be able to live up to my mom's standards. My dad and she spent a few days apart and then talked about their expectations, which weren't major. My mom asked him to be baptized Greek Orthodox. No problem. My mom knew Dad wasn't the most romantic person in the world. Fine. Once they realized that they did want the same thing, they had a double wedding with my mom's brother and his wife on June 10, 1951.

After a few years in New York City, they got a call from my mom's sister and her husband, who'd moved to Los Angeles. So they loaded up the truck and they moved to Beverly . . . I mean, Hollywood. Swimming pools, movie stars, and the beginnings of a family. My mom was pregnant with my sister soon after arriving. Three and a half years after that, I was born, and then, two years later, my brother.

On the weekends, my dad would pile us all into the Batmobile, a 1950-something black Plymouth convertible with a push-button transmission, and take us to Griffith Park, in the shade of the Griffith Observatory, for his weekly volleyball game. My mom would wrangle us to fill jugs with water from a spout emerging from a stone wall that was supposedly "spring" water. Hey, in Greece, water came out of a spring, so why not in Hollywood? At home after the game, my dad would barbecue, Greek-style (no Southern barbecue sauce for us, only oregano, garlic, and lemon), and as the sun set, we kids would watch TV as my parents cleaned up.

I never remember my parents complaining. I never heard either of them say they were tired, or bored, or mad. I remember my dad saying "God bless America" practically every day of my life. I remember my dad and his brother building an addition to our house one summer while we decamped to Oceanside to get away from the dusty construction. I remember my mom sewing our bedspreads, curtains, and clothes and cooking Greek food but also making peanut-butter-and-jelly sandwiches in an attempt to assimilate. I remember my parents laughing together.

Not only did my parents laugh, they cracked us up, too. My mom would do impersonations of all the kids in the neighborhood. (You haven't lived until you've heard a Greek immigrant lady say "bitchin'.") My dad had his own special talents. On one outing to the zoo, as we came upon the hyena cage, he started howling like a wolf and made the hyenas howl back at him. We could not believe that there, in the middle of Los Angeles, my dad was making hyenas talk to him. So my mom could imperson-ate kids and my dad could impersonate animals. We were like a Disney movie with an accent.

And now I'm here in the car on a Sunday, thinking, *Who knew? My mom pretended to be happy all these years. Now she is saying maybe she made a mistake?* I remember something else she recently said: "You know how they say, 'Opposites attract'? Well, later on, opposites attack!"

I tell my husband to make a left, not follow the car in front too closely (not that I'm bossy), and ask my mom what exactly she means.

She says, "Don't get me wrong. I love your dad. I always have. We created a beautiful life together, and I wouldn't change a thing, but now I know that I like to talk. When I was younger, I didn't know how much I needed that. I didn't really think about things like 'Will he watch *The Ed Sullivan Show* with me?' We both just wanted to have a good life and healthy kids. Back then, people married for life. Do I wish we had long, soulful talks? Sure. If I had known then that I needed that, I may have chosen a different kind of person, but I also knew he was a very good man."

My parents didn't demand from each other what we seem to demand today from our relationships. My dad loved sports but didn't insist she be on the golf course handing him his driver. Instead, he taught my sister and brother to play. My mom didn't complain about his lack of conversation; she found other outlets. She had us kids, her friends, and her extended family.

My parents knew it was all right if not every single one of their needs was being met by the other, because commitment to the life they shared and created was a bigger reward than anything else. So what if my dad wasn't clued in on the latest gossip? Or that my mom was perfectly okay never learning to ride a bike or swim? (I venture to say that my mom never exercised because she had to escape from her village during the war by hiking—at night, by herself—over some seriously steep mountains. I think she just thought, *That's pretty much it for exercise for the rest of my life.*)

As we pull up to the church, my parents are laughing and humorously harassing each other. My dad is helping my mom out of the car. The boys are helping my dad help my mom. I let my parents walk ahead, and as Dad guides Mom toward the church, I ask myself, *Would I ever want two other people as my parents?* The answer is immediate: Not me!

I start to understand that as my siblings and I grew up, so did my mom. And my dad. Their new country allowed them the choices they may not have had in their home-lands, where my mom would have likely married a pre-selected groom, as her older sister had, and my dad probably would have married the local girl from his village because she was there. My parents were able to choose each other. God knows, a lot of women have made some foolish choices in their past (stop staring at me!). What if my mom had gotten what she now thinks she wanted, a "talker"? What if that talker was also a gambler, a drunk, a cheat? I doubt that guy would still be in the car going to church with his kids and grandkids. So I look at these two "opposites" and think, *They're still attracting each other.* The magnet of their lives still has a pretty strong pull. I turn to look back at my husband, who is locking the car, and take his hand.

Strings Attached

April Wilder

Mid-divorce, my soon-to-be-ex-husband and I stood teary-eyed in an airport, boarding planes bound for the separate cities housing our newly separated lives, wondering how we would "stay friends"—but actually really do it. I joked that we should have a child to guarantee lifelong contact. Four years later (jokesters, beware), we did just that, the statistically freakish result of a one-night stand.

The act itself can be blamed on the usual antecedents: a wedding, an open wine cellar, a tent. The wedding was my sister's; my ex was invited because he was still tight with my father and because I needed a buffer from the difficult woman my father had recently married. To wit, when we arrived, we were shown not to a room in the house I grew up in, but to a tent my poor, torn father had pitched outside in the yard, as if we were displaced hurricane survivors. Not one to let such a slight go unadvertised, I dragged an old, unmounted door from the garage and propped it against the tent, demanding that anyone wanting to speak with either T or me knock first. After the reception, T and I listed back to the tent and fell into the door, which fell into the tent, wherein we promptly forgot we weren't married.

On the mightily hungover ride to the airport the next day, we admitted to not feeling all that guilty. We both were seeing other people—T was living with a woman—but with an ex-spouse, it sort of seems like you've got a freebie coming.

A few weeks after the wedding, I started feeling sick. I went to the doctor and told her the only thing that occurred to me: "It looks like I'm in menopause, so you'll have to give me whatever you give people for that."

She left, came back, and said that this was the opposite of menopause.

I called a friend and made her chain-smoke in my backyard while I sat downwind and cried, ankle-deep in the sun-bright leaves of a Utah fall. I was forty-one, a hermit-writer who slept ten to twelve hours a night, a tomboy who had held perhaps two babies, ever, regarding them as benign, ignorable life-forms on the order of cats. We talked about my options, sort of, but I understood that if this late in the game a baby was going to fall out of the sky into my unlikely lap, then I needed to do as I was told, so to speak, and have it.

When my friend left, I steeled myself and called T. His first reaction was a sound effect, the *ooouff* you hear when someone catches a hard-thrown ball in the gut. Then he said, "Okay. Let me think. We've got to think."

I told him I'd already tried that, and it wasn't helping.

"How sure are they?"

"They seem pretty sure. In the hundreds percent."

After T, I called the guy I'd been dating before the wedding, who also could have been the father, a cheeky/dorky ordained Buddhist something or other (I thought of him as "the monk") from a Zen sect that lets you keep all your money. The monk came around to the idea in that one phone call—and even started sounding happy about it—despite the paternity issue. "Don't worry about that now," he said. "Just breathe." This is why it hadn't worked out with us—his solicitude over things (breathing) that my body did automatically. I liked his company, though; he was calming and kind and can-do. A few weeks later, he flew out from New Jersey to accompany me to the first ultrasound.

According to the ultrasound tech, the baby's measurements put her (her?!) at thirteen-ish weeks old, which would mean she'd preexisted my sister's wedding by two weeks, thus ruling out T as the father. Together the monk and I sat absorbing this news in the genetic counselor's office, a room so small it seemed like a gag. We could have easily shaken the woman's hand, left, and never questioned paternity again. But as we were standing to go, I for some reason asked, "So that's a solid date, right? Thirteen weeks?"

The doctor started to nod; then her expression wilted like someone who's just remembered she has no friends. "Or—wait. No. It's not necessarily solid."

So began our adventure with the pregnancy calculator, a small cardboard disk with a central arrow like on a carnival wheel of fortune. "Without going into too much detail," I explained, "I need to rule out one particular night as the conception date in order to know the baby is ours."

The doctor smiled down at the wheel, its arrow pointing to the day of my sister's wedding. "But this is the likeliest day, given your cycle. I mean, really, that's the day."

"But that's eleven weeks ago, not thirteen."

"That's definitely the day, though. Let me see if someone else can explain this better."

At some point in the pageant of medical professionals who squeezed into the clown car of an office to explain how this baby could be thirteen weeks old even though she'd been conceived at some point that was not thirteen weeks ago, the monk and I conceded to the power of the wheel. His hand went slack in mine as he—extremely uncharacteristically—snapped at one of the doctors: "We're not idiots. We get it." In the parking garage, he stood by my open car window, saying, "You know I'll always take care of you guys, right? No matter what, I'll always be there. Tell me you know that." I looked at him, the smudges on his glasses. I was surprised to hear him talk that way at our age.

Tryingly, it would be two more months before a prenatal

paternity test could resolve the matter absolutely, months that included Christmas, New Year's, Valentine's Day. Until then, we just had to wait—T in San Diego, the monk in New Jersey, my rapidly expanding self in Salt Lake City. T kept his secret close, telling no one, slogging through his days in a fog of dissonance. The monk, on the other hand, showed my daughter's ultrasound pictures to strangers in coffee shops and regularly flew back and forth between Jersey and Salt Lake to make sure, as promised, that I/we were taken care of.

When the time came, he found a genetic testing center in a strip mall, a colorless hive of cubicles where a man named Ricardo bore witness as the monk swabbed a Q-tip around his inner cheek. We had a two-week wait for the results, a time I passed in a fever of Darwinian analysis: Who would be the better father from a petri-dish perspective? One was more athletic, the other had nicer teeth; neither could dance, but one could sing; one fidgeted, the other had a rather feminine walk; each was smart and kind, but one was more of both. Knowing me as he did, T would text me things like, "I bet you're drooling over my genes," and I would think, *Okay, he's funnier; the funnier one should be the dad.* But T didn't want children, while the monk wanted one in abundance. Were he the father, I knew, my single motherhood would be half as hard.

On the fourteenth day, Ricardo called and left an almost sadistically circuitous message in which, at the last possible moment, he disclosed that the monk was not a match. When I got the news, I was teaching a fiction class at the U. on the hill. We had been workshopping a monologue written from the point of view of a cow. I told my students, "Some of you are trying way too hard here. Don't think you have to sit around making stuff up. Your normal lives are weird enough. Trust me."

Because it seemed more urgent to deliver yes-news than no-news, I called T first. He didn't sound surprised in the least.

I said, "Can you say something positive about all of this?"

"Of course. I've just got a lot to figure out, but I know she'll be beautiful."

"But do you want her, like, *at all?*"

"Of course, baby," he said. He hadn't called me "baby" in a long time, and though there was no question of our reuniting (it had taken many years and all our combined strength to get divorced), it was hard not to feel endeared toward a relationship that was apparently harder to leave than the Mafia. "Listen to me," he said. "I'm not going to leave you hanging on this." I knew that this was so, but I also knew that "I won't leave you hanging" was a far cry from "I want this." When we hung up, I realized I'd half expected him to say he'd be flying out so we could sit and plan; I thought he'd want to feel the baby kick, because that would make it real. But he hadn't offered to do any of those things—didn't even want to see ultrasound pictures.

Next I called the monk and told him, "It's not the answer you want." As I spoke, I saw myself sitting in my bungalow growing pregnanter and pregnanter without his calls, texts, pep talks, and visits. I thought about the day I was walking my dogs and a guy leaned out of a slowing car and yelled, "Where's that baby's daddy? Why isn't he out here walking those dogs?"

Last I called my father, who said, "Isn't that wonderful!"

"No, Dad, it's not. T will do what's right, but he doesn't *want* this."

"That doesn't matter right now. It's the disposition that's important."

I sighed. "I don't know how I made such a mess of things."

"A mess?" he said. "Life by design is a mess. The minute you're born, you're dying." I heard him puffing on a cigar. "I don't pretend to know what drives you in this world, but you don't apologize to nobody for nothing."

T delayed telling his girlfriend about the baby, because they had been planning a fancy trip to Europe. "I know she'll probably leave me," he said sadly, "so I'd at least like to go on our trip and tell her when we get back."

I said, "Your only shot at keeping her is to confess and then immediately propose."

"Yeah, that's every girl's dream: 'Hey, I knocked up my ex-wife. Will you marry me?'"

"It was just a one-night stand," I said.

"A one-night stand that's going to walk and talk and never go away."

A week or so after they returned from Europe, he texted me at 6:00 A.M.: "It's done. I told her. Don't know how I could have hurt that girl more than I have."

She packed up and stayed with friends for a week. Then, to everyone's surprise, she returned, somehow willing to see what could be salvaged between them.

I sat in the stripped backyard of late winter and tried to think what our futures would look like. I didn't doubt that T would take care of the baby financially, but at this point money was the least of my worries. By nature I'm a low-energy person. When I tried to imagine even just bending to pick the baby up, I would see, as in a commercial for assisted living, a stray hand shoot to my lower back, hear a deep moan as my knees buckled. It was also becoming clear that T wouldn't say or do anything not approved by the girlfriend he was scrambling to keep. A ground rule of their probationary reunion was that T and I never be alone together. This meant T could come to the birth only if his girlfriend came, to which—during the last two hot, bloated, bitchy, scary, sleepless months—I wrote and called and texted "*NO.*"

At semester's end, my students finally asked about the pregnancy. They wanted to know if I would write about it. I wasn't quite sure what to say. I was due in a few weeks, and already I felt shady in public, like everyone was looking me over, wondering who I thought I was and where exactly I'd come by this baby. I wondered these things myself. I didn't even know when I would see T again, but since my students wanted to hear about him, and since it was a writing class, I found myself telling them about our first married years, when I would follow T around our apartment with awful, horrible early drafts of stories and novels and read aloud to him during *Monday Night Football* commercial breaks. We both had math backgrounds and knew nothing about the stuff I was trying to write. He'd hand back a few hundred pages and say, "I can't tell if that character's stuck in a bathtub or a taxicab." But he believed, or seemed to, that if I just kept going, eventually a shape would appear in the chaos.

I didn't know, as I stood trying to explain things to my class, that a week after our daughter's birth, T and his girlfriend would fly out to meet her. Or that by six months, they'd be seeing her regularly, with me flying her to San Diego and staying in a hotel or, for longer visits, turning right around and flying home on the same plane. I had no reason to believe, back then, that our funny little family would ever spend more than a few airport minutes together at a time, and I certainly had nothing to prepare me for the afternoon of my daughter's second Halloween, when her father—newly broken up with his girlfriend—would spontaneously get on an airplane to take her trick-or-treating.

When my ex-brother-in-law learned we were expecting a baby, he emailed me: "Why am I not surprised? You guys never did anything the normal way." This was true. Fifteen years earlier, T had asked me out over a dot-matrix printer at work; for our first date, he took me to see *Blue Velvet* at the Brew & View in Chicago. We sat at a wobbling cocktail table and drank Pabst Blue Ribbon and made each other laugh, and he leaned forward and smiled the way his daughter does now—the way she did that Halloween, strutting between us in a peacock costume and holding our hands, every few feet jumping into a swing, landing, and looking up to confirm that we were really both there at once, together but apart, a trick and a treat.

Divorce Dreams

Ellen Tien

————✢————

I contemplate divorce every day.

It tugs on my sleeve each morning when my husband, Will, greets me in his chipper, smug, morning-person voice, because after sixteen years of waking up together, he still hasn't quite pieced out that I'm not viable before 10:00 A.M.

It puts two hands on my forehead and mercilessly presses when he blurts out the exact wrong thing ("Are you excited for your surprise party next Tuesday?"); when he lies to avoid the fight ("What do you mean I left our apartment door open? I never even knew our apartment *had* a door!"); when he buttons his shirt and jacket into the wrong buttonholes, collars and seams unaligned like a vertical game of dominoes, with possibly a scrap of shirttail zippered into his fly. It flicks me, hard, just under the eye when, during a parent-teacher conference, he raises his arm high in the air, scratches his armpit, and then—*then!*—absently smells his fingers.

It slammed into me like a four-thousand-pound Volvo station wagon one spring evening four years ago, although I remember it as if it were last year. He had dropped me off in front of a restaurant prior to finding a parking spot. As I crossed in front of the car, he pulled forward, happily smiling back over his left shoulder at some random fascinating bit (a sign with an interesting font, a new scaffolding, a diner that he may or may not have eaten at the week after he graduated from college), and plowed into me. The impact, while not wondrous enough to break bodies twelve ways, was sufficient to bounce me sidewise onto the hood, legs waving in the air like antennae, skirt flung somewhere up around my ears.

For one whole second, New York City stood stock-still and looked at my underwear.

As I pounded the windshield with my fist and shouted—"Will, Will, stop the car!"—he finally faced forward, *blink*,

blink, blink, trying, yes, truly trying to take it all in. And I heard him ask with mild astonishment, very faintly because windshield glass is surprisingly thick, "What are you doing here?"

In retrospect, it was an excellent question, a question that I've asked myself from altar to present, both incessantly and occasionally.

What am I doing here?

Don't misunderstand: I would not, could not disparage my marriage (not on a train, not in the rain, not in a house, not with a mouse). After 192 months, Will and I remain if not happily married, then steadily so. Our marital state is Indiana, say, or Connecticut—some red areas, more blue. Less than bliss, better than disaster. We are arguably, according to my wide-ish range of reference, Everycouple.

Nor is Will the Very Bad Man that I've made him out to be. Rather, like every other male I know, he is merely a Moderately Bad Man, the kind of man who will leave his longboat-sized shoes directly in the flow of our home's traffic so that one day I'll trip over them, break my neck, and die, after which he'll walk home from the morgue, grief-stricken, take off his shoes with a heavy heart, and leave them in the center of the room until they kill the housekeeper.

Still, beneath the thumpingly ordinary nature of our marriage—Everymarriage—runs the silent chyron of divorce. It's the scarlet concept, the closely held contemplation of nearly every woman I know who has children who have been out of diapers for at least two years and a husband who won't be in them for another thirty. It's the secret reverie of a demographic that freely discusses postpartum depression, eating disorders, and Ambien dependence (often all in the same sentence) with the plain candor of golden brown toast. In a let-it-all-hang-out culture, this is the given that stays tucked in.

This is the Mid-Wife Crisis.

Mind you, when I say Mid-Wife Crisis, I mean the middle-of-married-life kind, not the kind where you go to Yale to learn how to legally brandish a birthing stool. As one girlfriend remarked, it's the age of rage—a period of high irritation that lasts roughly one to two decades. As a colleague emailed me, it's the simmering underbelly of resentment, the six-hundred-pound mosquito in the room. At a juncture where we thought we should have unearthed some modicum of certainty, we are turning into the Clash: If I go will there be trouble? If I stay will it be double? Should I stay or should I go?

Our mothers knew better than to ponder such questions, at least not out loud in front of God and the hairdresser. They deliberately waited to reach the last straw until their children were grown and the house was paid for. At twenty-five, they were ladies with lady clothes and lady hairdos—bona fide adults, the astronauts' wives. By forty, they were relics.

But we, we with our twenty-first-century access to youth captured in a gleaming Mason jar with a pinked square of gingham rubber-banded over the top, we are still visually tolerable if not downright irresistible when we're thirty or thirty-five or forty. If you believe the fashion magazines—which I devoutly do—even fifty- and sixty-year-olds are (lick finger, touch to imaginary surface, make sizzle noise) pretty hot tickets.

And we are tickets with jobs and disposable income. If

we jump ship now, we're still attractive prospects who may have another shot at happiness. There's just that sticky wicket of determining whether eternal comfort resides in the tried-and-true or whether the untried will be truer.

Our mothers, so old too young, believed that marriage was the best they could get. We, the children of mothers who settled (or were punished for not settling), wonder: *Is this as good as it gets?*

Our mothers feared being left alone. We crave time alone. Alone-time is the new heroin.

What are we doing here?

We were groomed to think bigger and better—achievement was our birthright—so it's small surprise that our marriages are more freighted. Marriage and its cruel cohort, fidelity, are a lot to expect from anyone, much less from swift-flying us. Would we agree to wear the same eye shadow or eat in the same restaurant every day for a life-time? "Nay," cry the villagers, the echo answers "nay." We believe in our superhood. We count on it.

I recently stood by as a designer, a mother in her forties, announced to a group of women that she was divorcing her husband. The women's faces flickered with curiosity, support, recognition, and—could it be?—yearning. Not a one of us suggested that she try harder to make it work. No voice murmured, "What a shame."

Because it isn't a shame. Divorce is no longer the shame that spits stain upon womanly merit. Conventional wisdom decrees that marriage takes work, but it doesn't *take* work, it *is* work. It's a job—intermittently fulfilling and annoying, with not enough vacation days. Divorce is a job, too (with even fewer vacation days). It's a matter of weighing your options.

A friend once compared the prospect of leaving her husband to leaving her child's private school: The school wasn't entirely to her liking, but her daughter was happy there; it wasn't what she'd expected, but applying to other schools involved a lot of costly, complicated paperwork and the nagging uncertainty of whether another school would accept her and/or really be that much better.

Another friend viewed divorce as being akin to an extended juice fast: You're intrigued but skeptical, admiring yet apprehensive. Is it dangerous? Does it work? You're not completely sold, but then again, you could envision yourself attempting it down the road.

What this says to me (other than: My friends sure do come up with awfully good metaphors!) is that women don't view divorce as a scary, shadowy behemoth. It's an unpalatable yet manageable task that may or may not yield a better result.

Having choices is a cornerstone of strength: Choosers won't be beggars. "Thinking about divorce is kind of like living in New York City with its museums and theater and culture," a doctor friend of mine said. "You may never actually go to any of these places, but for some reason, just the idea that you could if you wanted to makes you feel better."

Maybe one day, marriage—like the human appendix, male nipples, or your pinky toes—will become a vestigial structure that will, in a millennium or two, be obsolete. Our great-great-great-grandchildren's grandchildren will ask each other in passing, "Remember marriage? What was its function again? Was it that maladaptive organ that intermittently produced gastrointestinal antigens and sometimes got so inflamed that it painfully erupted?"

Yes. Yes it was.

Until that day of obsolescence, we can confront the dilemma and acknowledge that once upon a time is the stuff of fairy tales. We can consider the choice—to marry or not marry or leave a marriage—a privilege.

The Halfway House

Jessica Ciencin Henriquez

Until recently, I lived on the top floor of a Harlem brownstone, my ex-husband lived on the bottom floor, and the neighbors between us were lawyers (not ours). We no longer shared a last name, but we did share our three-year-old son and a postman who left a rubber-banded stack of envelopes in our lobby each day. I'd flip through my ex's junk mail to find my student-loan statements. I didn't know if we'd ever get back together, but I did know he was eligible for a zero percent interest credit card.

When we married in 2012, we knew the risk of putting on wedding rings was that we might one day take them off. When that risk became our reality, we were determined, for our son's sake, to divorce differently. He refused to be a weekend-only father; I refused to be an ex-wife who communicated solely via voice mails or voodoo dolls. For two years, we shuffled our boy back and forth. We went to therapy separately and together and saw our marriage for what it was: mostly a failure.

I was starting a graduate program and needed a place near campus. We agreed that any extra minutes in my schedule should be spent with our son rather than on a subway. While apartment hunting, we stumbled upon a building with both a top and bottom floor for rent. The price was right, the light was good, and we were feeling optimistic. We signed one-year leases and thought, *How bad could it be?*

On move-in day, we sat on our stoop and tried to define a structure. We exchanged keys but promised not to peek. We agreed that romantic partners would not be invited over. Instead, we could get a hotel room (his suggestion) or remain celibate (mine). We knew boundaries would be blurry, but we vowed to keep a healthy distance.

It turned out that any distance, healthy or otherwise, was impossible. He heard when I came and went, my heels heavy on the forty-five steps between us. On nights I made dinner, he would call upstairs to say "Smells good," and

I'd bring down leftovers. Every night when he headed home from work, he'd text, "On my way; need anything?" I'd respond, "No, thanks." It took living together again to make me less dependent on him; it took us not being married for him to become more considerate of me.

Sometimes I'd watch him leave in a suit, knowing he'd dressed for another woman. Sometimes the housekeeper mixed our laundry (because she wanted to save water) and sneaked one of his shirts into my stack (because she wanted to save our relationship). If I was feeling nostalgic or lonely or both, I'd put it on, inhaling the lavender detergent, a trace of his cologne, and the sweet odor of our son's sweat. This is what our divorce smelled like. It was, to me, proof of a family intact.

There's a moment after a breakup when you're supposed to say goodbye and go in opposite directions. To do so, someone has to turn and start walking away. Neither of us did. We still wanted to bear witness to the other's life long after we'd asked a judge to grant us the freedom not to.

Our friends and family were confused and amused, wondering how it would end. I told them living together let me pursue my education and still be the mother I wanted to be. I didn't tell them that being my ex's neighbor made me miss being his wife. I told them that our living situation forced us to be kind and careful. I didn't tell them that this kindness and care erased much of the damage we'd done. I told them that of course it was messy and confusing. I didn't tell them that I would rather have a complicated life near him than a simpler one without him.

And when our leases were up, we let them go and searched for a new home together—a place where we could become the partners we were finally ready to be.

Meant to Be

Julie Orringer

In Yiddish, there's a word for it: *bashert*. The meaning is something like "intended": the person who was meant for you. We're not talking about a soul mate, though modern usage often spins it that way; the original meaning is more complicated. Your *basherter* or *basherte* won't always make you happy, and your life together won't always be easy. But there's a sense of rightness, of having landed where you're supposed to be.

For most of us, that certainty is hard to come by. Life is messy and multivalent. Circumstances conspire to challenge our relationships. Yet for that we can be grateful: Sometimes a challenge can make it clear to us that we're meant to leave a partnership. Other times our problems bring us closer.

How, then, do we know? What makes us certain? For my sister, the clue was a sense of quiet. She used to spend hours talking to her friends about guys—analyzing, deciphering, strategizing—but when she started seeing the man who became her husband, all of that stopped. She felt calm and confident enough just to let things play out. Similarly, a married friend says his dating years always felt like a struggle; that his instincts often turned out to be wrong. But with the woman he ended up marrying, he suddenly knew all the right things to say. His marriage involves work, of course, but now the work feels like swimming with the current instead of struggling upstream.

That friend also says you can tell a lot from the most ordinary moments: On an unexceptional night, when you've ordered pizza and you're watching movies in moth-holed sweaters and each other's socks, and you both have miserable colds, are you happy? Are you exactly where you want to be?

Another friend—one who told me in an awed tone, three weeks after she met her future husband, "I'm going to marry that man"—says it's all about how you fight. In the midst of your worst arguments, the ones where you threaten and accuse and generalize and ungenerously compare, bringing up events buried years ago and slitting your eyes in disgust—at those moments, can you step back and perceive your ridiculousness? Can you remember why you like each other, even when you disagree? That principle inspired the best wedding present my husband and I received: a set of Groucho Marx glasses/noses/mustaches to be donned in moments of marital discord.

It's been twenty years since I met my husband and fourteen since we were married. In that time we've navigated uneven success, unforeseen disappointments, moments of shameful pride. We've lost a mother and a father between us; we've lived in six cities, worked countless jobs, survived autoimmune disease and smoking cessation. We've lost six pregnancies and given birth to a son. And in times of both euphoria and despair, there's no one I would rather have at my side than my husband. Not only because he knows how to celebrate and to comfort, but also because without him no joy or sorrow would have meaning.

In our marriage, we feel the sense of calm my sister describes; we feel, too, the relief of swimming with the current, the joys of small things. We watch movies in holey sweaters and old socks, and when we fight, we don our Groucho glasses and get through it. But it's that last something—that sense of deep partnership in the best and worst times—that makes me know I'm with the right person, that makes me sure this marriage is, in every sense of the word, *bashert*.

Can I Handle the Hard Times?

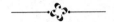

Miracles sometimes happen, but more often they're
made of faith and wit and hope and imagination,
to say nothing of sweat.

—Tom Waldman

Feel Your Feelings

Katie Arnold-Ratliff

Maybe you can experience levity enough to laugh, embarrassment enough to blush, irritation enough to bitch. But maybe the sadder, angrier, uglier stuff you drown out or deny. Maybe your life's central trauma, the biggie, the time when you were seventeen and a person who was supposed to protect you, whom you loved and still love, hurt you worse than you knew was possible—maybe you lock that up, turn from it. And why not? Those feelings are too big, too loud, unwieldy, undignified. Plus, that was ages ago. Plus, you have a life! And there's no room in it to nurse some old ache. So you tell yourself you're not wounded or enraged—everything is okay; don't look over there; nothing is happening over there—and soon all that anger and grief retreat. And opting out is so compelling, a study in clean, anesthetic ease.

But after a while you notice that you sure do watch a lot of TV, and change the subject all the time, and you're always ordering three whiskeys instead of one. You find that even your treasured relationships feel bloodless and rote. You find that you can't bear to be still because then you have to think.

So, though it makes you sweaty with fear, you sit down with a shrewd therapist, and she coldcocks you with this little number: "Nobody gets to block out the bad stuff without also losing the good." And after days of pissy denial, you see that she's right, that not feeling feelings worked *too* well! You don't have to suffer pain, but you've also lost out on its opposite. You're getting by on a low-fat, xeroxed, Muzak version of happiness. You see that you've become a liar, saying things like "I'm not hurt," "I'm not mad," "I'm fine." You grasp that these lies make you unknowable, which means no one really knows you, which means you're alone. You realize that when you refuse to feel pain, you wind up feeling it forever; you finance it, setting up an installment plan to buy decades of chronic anguish.

You decide to stop paying. You resolve to feel your feelings, starting with the big ones you've backlogged. (You gather you'll be hanging out with that shrewd therapist a while.) You look a friend in the eye and say an impossible thing, like "That hurts my feelings." You marvel when he apologizes, says he's glad you told him, that you always should. You file this away, acclimating to the bracing sensation of telling the truth. You take up a doofy hobby—pure fun, zero nutritional value—to remember what delight feels like. You think about the people you'd take a bullet for, square your shoulders, and tell them you love them, because in all this time you never have.

You fly home and invite the person who hurt you so bad, the person you loved and still love, into your pristine rental car. You don't have a destination in mind, but you want to be driving, holding the wheel, when you say another impossible thing, which is "You nearly broke me in half." And you marvel this time, as well—not because she, too, apologizes, though that is more than you knew you could hope for. No, you marvel because it doesn't matter what comes out of her mouth, because all that matters is that you have arrived somewhere. What matters is that you are awake and alive, you can see. You see that you still have time, you didn't waste it all. You see that you are strong enough to survive the world and the hurt floating around in it. And you see that ditching a way of life that did you no favors—that made you a stranger to yourself, left you only a partial person—feels really good.

Not to Look Away

Marie Howe

———❦———

Ten minutes into my friend Jason's funeral, the rabbi's cell phone started ringing. Jason would have told that joke a thousand times. But his body lay in the coffin, and now we tell the joke.

Is this what a story can do? Emerge from the most painful event and transform it into something else? So sad. So funny. Both. And life is there, for a moment, almost adequately represented.

I'm looking for the gate, Jason used to say when he was in pain. I can't find the gate, but I'm looking. What was this gate my friend Jason was looking for? Maybe he wanted to find the door in the room of suffering, so that he might walk through it into another story. If my being in pain would relieve someone else, Jason said, then I would bear it gladly. I want to be present, he used to say. That's all we can be, he would say, present—and kind.

How difficult it is to be present. A few weeks ago, in one of those drooling late-night states trolling through the emails, exhausted, depleted, clicking through the internet, I clicked on a link that promised to show me Angelina Jolie's split leather pants. Before the page materialized, I turned off the computer and put my head in my hands. And in the sudden quiet of the dark apartment—the blue screen extinguished, the radiator hissing, my eight-year-old sleeping—I noticed death and life sitting quietly beside me, waiting for my attention. Jason's death and my own.

Oh, who wouldn't want to look away? The cell phone rings, another singer on TV is belting it out, and the glittering Web beckons like the Milky Way in a box—promising that if I keep clicking and clicking, I might finally get to what I long for, to the message, the rug, the T-shirt. I will move beyond suffering and beyond time, beyond the limits of my money and my story and life.

But that place? It's not there—it's virtual—it's nowhere. The days and nights of my life walk by, arm in arm with time, and the gate to the new story stands just outside the circle of my attention. Sometimes I lie here, Jason said, and walk through the old house of my childhood, through all the rooms, and look out all the windows.

This might be the most difficult task for us in postmodern life: not to look away from what is actually happening. To put down the devices. To look long enough so that we can look through them—like a window. Jason looked up one day last week and said, This is unendurable. Then he said, I like that black sweater.

How do we learn this kind of attention? A lot of his friends were with Jason during his life and the last three years of his illness. Everyone has stories. Lucie told us this one. She picked up Jason from the hospital and drove all night to get to Provincetown; he wanted to go there for maybe the last time. Walking slowly through the fog on the beach in the very early morning she said, We will always remember this day. And Jason, who was pretty well practiced by then, said, I am remembering it now.

You Can See

Thich Nhat Hanh

———◆———

When you feel anger coming—like a storm rising up from the bottom of your consciousness—turn your focus to your breath. Breathe in deeply to bring your mind home to your body. Then look at or think of the person triggering this anger: With mindfulness, you can see that she is unhappy, that she is suffering. You can see her wrong perceptions. You can see that she is not beautiful when she says things that are unkind. You can also see that you don't want to be like her. You'll feel motivated by a desire to say or do something nice—to help the other person suffer less. This means compassionate energy has been born in your heart. And when compassion appears, anger is deleted.

My Mother's Daughter

Bonnie Jo Campbell

I can milk a cow, castrate a pig, stack hay in a barn, and shovel manure into the back of a truck all afternoon. I can change a tire in the rain, brew elderberry wine, and create chocolate candies using my granny's old recipes and black walnuts I've picked up along the road. Early in life, I decided to be a person who could do anything, and when I wanted to travel and had no money, I hitchhiked across the continent. Once, I bicycled over the highest pass in the Swiss Alps, carrying my sleeping bag, luggage, bike tools, and food.

At age forty, in order to be able to defend myself, I took up martial arts and earned a second-degree black belt in Kobudo, an Okinawan weapons art. Nowadays I also run several times a week, to stay in shape, for sure, but also so

I'll be able to outrun an attacker or chase down a runaway child before she wanders into the road. I've taught my nieces how to pee in the woods (instead of trying to balance with your panties down, lean your back against a tree as though sitting in a chair). You might say I've made it my business not to be helpless, whether that means learning how to patch the roof, snake out the drain, or install ceramic tile to save money and the trouble of hiring someone. Refusing to be helpless has made me a better wife and companion to my husband of twenty-six years. He knows he can rely on me to do my share and shoulder whatever burdens our lives present.

My spirit of self-sufficiency has come largely from my mother, Susanna, who raised five children alone and learned to butcher her own animals in order to feed us, despite having an arm that was damaged at birth, leaving her partially disabled. She has always loved men, but she never wanted to depend on one.

Now that my mother is aging, I see her needing more help, and it frightens me. She's just had her second spinal surgery and is recovering in a determined way, but she's very restricted in her movements. Every day she makes a list of the tasks that are beyond her; a recent list included "clean up the cat's vomit" and "take the lid off the cranberry juice." This is the woman who canned two hundred quarts of tomatoes every autumn and saddle-broke wild horses in her spare time. She didn't tolerate slacking in her kids and was maybe even more demanding of my sister and me than of my three brothers, since she knew the pitfalls that await women who can't take care of themselves. We heard about the dangers of alcohol, men, and pregnancy years before we needed to.

Though Susanna has had her share of difficult and sorrowful circumstances, she has rarely asked for sympathy. Yet she has always been quick to offer it. When she had money beyond what the bills required, she often loaned it out with little hope of repayment. She allowed other kids to move into our house to avoid abusive or difficult homes, and after her own kids left home, she rented the rooms cheaply to folks in need. In other words, all the while she was being tough, my mother was cultivating a life rich with friends and family who are now eager to help her when she can't do everything herself. Her new challenge is learning how to let them.

Come What May

Joan Silber

My father, a hardworking dentist who loved to read and play pinochle, died of a heart attack when I was five and my mother was in her late thirties. My mother had a strategy for facing the world: She didn't believe in luck; she believed in sturdiness. Though we spent years at odds, even I (her most critical witness) had to admire this. Strength was her plan B.

While this approach failed to make certain human concessions—she disapproved of weeping at funerals, sang a soap-opera theme song if she thought I was overdramatizing—I have come to regard it as one of the gifts of my upbringing. I don't mean (who would believe me if I did?) that I've always behaved well in the face of disaster. But I had a model of hardiness to copy, standards to pull me through. A plan B, whatever its parameters, assumes not only that catastrophe will strike, but also that a person can be equal to it.

As a kid, I often imagined possible tests. "If an enemy army took over, would you deny your beliefs? Would you betray someone if it got really bad?" These rehearsals showed a desire to be ready for the worst, a wish to be fearless.

Some of the happier memories of my childhood are the times when the lights went out. Hurricanes can hit New Jersey in the fall, and we were always ready. Flashlights, candles, food, blankets. During one storm, my older brother put a birthday candle in the candlestick from the game Clue, which I thought was incredibly witty. Lack of panic made us festive.

I live in Manhattan now, and when Hurricane Sandy hit in 2012, I was stocked with bottled water, a filled tub, and enough dog food for weeks. I try to remember that my carry-on, however minimal, had better contain a nightgown, a toothbrush, and underwear, just in case the airline loses my luggage. Who can say it won't?

What Really Matters?

If I were to wish for anything I should not wish for
wealth and power but for the passionate sense
of the potential. . . .

—Søren Kierkegaard

Yes and No

Valerie Monroe

No, you do not have to wash your hair every day; only when it's dirty. But, yes, you must wash your face every night—though it's fine just to rinse in the morning. Yes, you should always send a card or an email or call after a dinner party. No, you don't have to apologize for disagreeing. No, you don't have to have curtains—or table settings for eight (or even four). No, you don't need a signature fragrance. Yes, there is lead in your lipstick—but not enough to harm you, unless you're eating fifteen tubes a day. What's the healthiest thing to have first thing in the morning? A stretch and some fruit. (And also gratitude. And right before bed? More gratitude.) No, you don't need to brush your hair, except to style it. Yes, you do want to think twice about anything you post on social media. No, you don't have to answer the phone whenever it rings. Yes, it's fine not to know what comes next; you'll figure it out. It's also fine to wear your hair at any length you please, no matter your age. Yes, you should probably get a skin-cancer check once a year. And, yes, you must know where your money is—and double-check that you know for sure. No, you don't want to compare, because comparing is the death of happiness. But, yes, you might want to compete, because in the right context (a Flywheel class, say) competition can be very motivating. Yes, you can be dear friends with your exes. Yes, you do have to forgive your parents, but first you have to forgive yourself. And: Yes, you can; yes, you will; *yes*.

Finders, Keepers, Hoarders, Weepers

Michelle Herman

I'd like to say it was the mice that pushed me over the edge. It *should* have been the mice. But I ignored the evidence of their presence just as I ignored the towers of books and papers, the mountains of stuff everywhere.

Housekeeping has never been high on my priority list. By last spring, though, it had been years since I'd so much as glanced that far down the list. Even with the things a person needs to do to keep her family alive and non-naked, I was cutting corners, stopping on my way home from teaching a class to buy more underwear for all of us because that was easier than doing laundry. I had given up keeping house altogether.

Okay, not *altogether*. I was still making a token effort at tidying—stacking my daughter's schoolwork, my students' papers, my own manuscripts, books, magazines, news-papers, and junk mail, and throwing small items (a watch with a broken strap, a stray battery or key) into one big bowl or basket or another. But the stacks were turning into heaps, the bowls and baskets had begun to multiply, and by last spring, every surface in the house seemed to be covered. The top of the upright piano was piled with leaning towers of sheet music, and next to the towers was a jumble of things I had set down "just for now." To eat dinner, we had to shove aside stacks of papers to make room for plates and elbows on the table. And in my study—once a sacrosanct place, a writer's haven—I had to pick my way through shopping bags that bulged with my thirteen-year-old daughter's outgrown clothes and piles of laundry I had managed to wash and dry but not put in drawers. In the closet, there were cardboard boxes full of memorabilia, manuscripts, letters, and Grace's baby things, her schoolwork, artwork, and picture books.

And the closet was just for the things that had to stay clean and dry. Everything else we were saving was in the basement—a room I did my best to avoid. I didn't go down there unless I had to—and when I did, I kept my eyes trained straight ahead. I walked right by my husband's bed from before he moved in with me, and the two sets of rusting darkroom equipment and the many bottles of seeping darkroom chemicals. I didn't even glance at my daughter's disassembled crib and changing table and high chair, every bike she'd ever owned, two car seats and two booster seats, the plastic potty, the playpen, three broken vacuum cleaners, the motorcycle helmet, the space heater, and two window fans. I ignored the half dozen battered suitcases, some with broken zippers. The old tent. The four glass aquarium tanks. The grass skirt on a hanger, dangling from a pipe. The two shopping bags full of empty baby-food jars in which once upon a time I had frozen my breast milk.

Later, when I hired someone to help me deal with all of this, she would look around the basement and ask me, genuinely curious, "Have you ever thrown anything out?"

"You mean, other than actual trash?" I said.

She opened her mouth to say something, then closed it again. Her eyes were full of pity.

By spring things were so bad, even my husband noticed—and housekeeping isn't even *on* his priority list.

When he finishes a fourteen-hour day of painting in his studio, he sleeps; when he wakes up, the last thing he wants to do is clean—and who can blame him?

Well, I did, of course. When he'd first moved in with me, he had said he would keep house. It was only fair, he said, if he was going to be painting at home full time while I was writing and teaching. I agreed, ignoring the fact that even if he had cared about keeping things tidy, he would have had no idea how to go about it. When he'd first started spending time at my house and I complained that he never put anything away, he said, plaintively, "But where is 'away'?"

It was easier to do it myself. Then it was easier not to do it at all.

Toward what she believed was the end of her life—although she actually lived another fourteen years—my grandmother started going through her belongings. You couldn't leave her apartment without being given something to take away: "You always liked this, didn't you? Take it." We felt awful carting off the things she didn't want anymore. But I think we misread her. When she gave me the cookie tin full of buttons I'd played with as a girl, she wasn't saying she didn't want to remember our time together; when she gave me the notebook in which she'd practiced writing English, she wasn't saying she wanted to forget the night-school classes she'd finally taken the year I was thirteen. By thrusting things into my hands, she was just making sure they got into the *right* hands, that they weren't discarded after she'd held on to them so long.

When she did die, in her nineties, there was still plenty of stuff in her apartment. I was in Columbus, Ohio, with a newborn baby; it fell to my mother to go to the apartment in Brooklyn and figure out what was worth keeping. She couldn't do it. It was too hard. She couldn't bear to put her hands on everything, to decide what was good, what was trash. She grabbed all the photographs and had my father call the Institute of Jewish Humanities to take the rest.

The woman I ended up hiring to help me get control of my home does a lot of work cleaning out houses after people have died and their children can't deal with the sorting. She says my mother did pretty well—and my grandmother very well indeed. She sometimes goes into people's houses with their children, who look around and after a few minutes say, "Throw everything away." She can't stand that. There are all those photographs everywhere, and she knows that buried in drawers, in cabinets, in boxes, there must be letters, truly meaningful things mixed in with the receipts and grocery lists. But it's too hard for people to separate the meaningful from the meaningless; they'd rather dispense with it all.

That's where I was heading. I didn't want to go there. I just didn't know it yet.

And then something happened.

It wasn't anything dramatic. It was hardly anything.

My daughter and I were in Columbia, Missouri, for a wedding. My husband—who hates parties and hates to travel—was at home with the dog, the bird, the guinea pigs, and the mess. One of my best friends from graduate school lives in Columbia, and when Grace and I visited, I felt something tug at me: despair. Her living room was still an explosion of colors and textures, like in grad school, but now everything was better, *nicer*, than it had been when we didn't have any money.

Meanwhile, my house was worse, much worse, than the house I'd lived in during grad school.

"I can't believe we live this way," I told my husband when I got home.

"I can," he said.

"You can?"

"I mean, I can believe *I* live this way. I just can't believe you do."

It was as if a bomb went off in my head.

I called a friend who has lived in Columbus all her life and whom I can always count on to know "the best" of whatever I'm in need of. The next morning, Terra Marzetti (*Terror?* Grace asked, alarmed. No, I told her: *Terra,* the earth) walked through my house with me, not saying a word as I chattered nervously. When she did speak, she was matter-of-fact. "You realize that this house is infested with mice."

Infested? I coughed out a laugh. Not *infested.* I knew we had a few mice. I'd seen some droppings, I told Terra. I just hadn't gotten around to setting traps. But I would, I promised, right away.

It was too late for traps, Terra said gently. There were too many mice. And then she took me from room to room, moving furniture, moving stacks, opening drawers, showing me the nests—mice made nests?—and all the things the mice had ruined. I had to go out immediately and buy poison, she said.

It took five days for all the mice to die or flee, and by then Terra and I had gotten started. We worked side by side, ten hours a day, and I kept at it even after she left each evening, until I collapsed, past midnight.

Friday, Saturday, Sunday, Monday, Tuesday.

Terra, who called herself a home-space orchestrator, was systematic and patient, working room by room, sorting every single thing she saw into one of three categories: obviously trash, obviously good, and look it over and decide. When I'd sorted the look-it-over piles into one or the other of the first two categories, I hauled out the trash and then contemplated what was left so I could make more decisions: good and keep, or good and give away? I filled bag after bag with clothes and toys and linens to donate to Goodwill. Meanwhile, Terra cleaned.

In my study, a lot of things had been ruined by mice

and had to be thrown away, but I still had to go through all the boxes the mice hadn't gotten to. I filled plastic bins (with lids that locked tight—Terra's rule) with the things I wanted to save: the journal, with illustrations, that Grace had kept the year she was six; notes from my friend Amy, who died; all my letters from my junior high school boyfriend, Howie; the novel I wrote when I was eleven; a few drawings of mine that my grandmother had saved and given back to me during those years of her own jettisoning. The notebook in which she practiced her English. The cookie tin full of buttons.

If I didn't do this, I told myself, eventually Grace would have to. Someone would have to. Or no one would—and everything would be chucked. That was what kept me going.

By Tuesday night, I had filled 360 fifty-gallon contractor's trash bags—a third for charity, two-thirds with trash. And we hadn't even gotten to the basement yet.

Terra hired a crew to clear out the basement. They came on Wednesday morning with a Dumpster big enough for a construction site. There were a few things that hadn't been ruined by years of storage in the damp—Grace's bikes and stroller, the space heater, an assortment of toys—and before the crew arrived, I hauled those things upstairs and put them in the charity pile or out in the alley, where I was sure someone would drive by and snatch them up (I was right). But the crib that might have been useful to someone was ruined after being in the wet basement for eleven years; the car seats were not only ruined but obsolete. Then there were all the things that should never have been saved to begin with—the broken suitcases, the baby-food jars.

I didn't watch the crew work; I couldn't. I stayed upstairs, going through file cabinets, filling bag after bag with paper to recycle—manuals for electronic devices I no longer owned, manuscripts of stories by people I hadn't talked to in eighteen years, AAA TripTiks for trips I'd made in 1986.

When, finally, unable to stand it anymore, I wandered downstairs, outside, the Dumpster was full: A mound rose out of the center of it—a mountain of trash. I watched the men throw things on top; I listened to glass break, to the thud of wood on wood, the clank of metal.

The leader of the little band of men, a great big man

named Alan, sweating and breathing hard, came up to me as I stood and watched, and put his hand on my shoulder. "This must be hard," he said softly. I burst into tears.

I still can't say exactly why I was saving all that stuff. Some of it was about a confusion of meaning—what matters and what doesn't—and my reluctance to make that distinction. Some of it was learned behavior: My grandmother, by her example, had taught me to save everything. In their way, my parents had, too. They saved nothing—none of my toys or clothes, not one volume of the Bobbsey Twins or Nancy Drew—and for years, I'd been making up for it.

But a lot of my hoarding was about "just in case": the fear that something would go wrong and I'd find myself in *need* of an old bed; a sense that it would be courting disaster to give up suitcases with broken zippers. I'd spent years, after deciding to make my way in the world as a writer, eking out a living, just barely getting by. There was a time when "a new pillow" was on my pie-in-the-sky wish list, when I'd dig through the crevices of my sole armchair for enough change to buy groceries with. My husband has been there, too—which is why, when I started to take the space heater to the alley, he balked. "That's a good space heater," he said. But we didn't need it, I pointed out (as much to myself as to him). We had a perfectly adequate furnace. And if the power went off, an electric space heater wouldn't do us any good, would it?

So: a combination of superstition, training, and over-correction of the past. A recipe for a house stuffed full, and a woman at the center of it, overwhelmed.

I don't suppose I will ever be the sort of person who lives a pared-down life, but I've made a lot of progress. I have put my hands on every single thing in the house—from all the clothes that had to be laundered in the mice's wake to every Playbill, baking pan, and slip of paper—and made a decision about it. I feel as if I have wrestled my possessions, and my house itself, to the ground. As if I have been through therapy—house therapy.

Terra, my house therapist, returns each week to help with cleaning—because I'm not kidding myself, I realize I have neither the time nor the inclination to keep things tidy on my own. Knowing that she's coming helps keep me vigilant: I do triage on everything that comes through the door, and if it's not something we need (now, for real—not maybe someday) or something that deserves to be saved for posterity, it's discarded. I stop before I let myself drop something into a drawer or set it down on the piano. "Where does it belong?" I think. If I don't have a place for it, I make one.

And it occurs to me that for the first time in years, it feels as if there is a place for *me* in my house. I like that I have chosen what surrounds me—that I choose, now, every day. It's what keeps me keeping house.

Give Yourself a Happiness Raise

Margarita Bertsos

———❧———

Last year, as I faced my thirty-third birthday, it seemed like a good time to sit down and make a list of financial goals. Some were instantly doable, like spending less on food. (Goodbye, seven-dollar organic strawberries.) Others were more ambitious: Sock away enough cash for a down payment on an apartment; build a savings account for fun grown-up stuff like buying last-minute plane tickets to Tahoe.

The problem: These things required more money than I was making. The other problem: In this economy, it wasn't realistic to expect a huge raise. Suddenly my future started to look like an ever-narrowing tunnel. Without a big increase in cash flow, how was my *amazing life* supposed to start?

I loved my job, I loved my boss, but I'd spent my twenties closing up shop at the office every night when I knew I should have been playing harder and taking more risks. I'd built a career I was proud of, but I realized I couldn't view a paycheck as my ultimate reward.

Finally I made an executive decision. I'd give myself a happiness raise and bring into my life more of the good things that money can't buy (and that I'd been denying myself) and less of the stuff that didn't have much real value.

The first step was to do a serious accounting, calculating where I'd been spending my time and energy and noting how much joy I was netting on a daily basis. The results didn't surprise me: so many have-tos and must-dos, so few moments of real bliss.

I instituted a new rule: Anytime the word "should" flashed across my mind, I hit the brakes. Did I really want to attend this baby shower or join that book club? Often I didn't—so I respectfully said no, and found that the world didn't end.

Then there was my health. I'd been trying to lose weight for years, and I'd had some success, but at the expense of my happiness (and my bank account). I dutifully joined a gym and then stopped going. Because that wasn't a big enough source of shame, I spent more money to join another—and didn't go there, either. I finally let myself admit that I hated boot-camp classes and pounding along a treadmill, so I quit and signed up for twelve-dollar Greek dancing lessons. I got back in the pool and swam laps, giving my body a taste of weightlessness. I also stopped counting the calories in blueberries. I threw out my scale. The result: I dropped four dress sizes. When I focused on pleasure in other areas of my life, I had less time to think about food and more desire to get up and move. And it wasn't torture—it was *fun*.

Once I stopped wasting energy on things I didn't want to do, I suddenly had headspace for all those things I used to say I didn't have time for, like a love life. The idea of dating—the thought of losing my independence, letting someone else see my imperfections—really scared me. But I pushed past the fear and created a profile on EligibleGreeks .com, the Match.com for Greek people. The first man who emailed me and didn't seem completely crazy lived across the country in Southern California. There was a time when

I would have let his message wither in my in-box. (He's from L.A.! Long distance never works! He wears those weird wraparound sunglasses!) But this time I wrote back.

We traded messages for a month, and then an unexpected work trip brought me to L.A. (Side note: When you invest in your happiness, the universe has a way of matching your contributions.) We planned to meet for dinner; I planned to have no expectations. But once I got over my initial nervousness, I talked more easily with him than I had with anyone I'd met in years. The night went so well, he asked me to extend my trip.

Our story didn't have a fairy-tale ending, but no matter. I had taken a risk and learned that if I needed to, I could get comfortable with being uncomfortable. Even more important, I realized something I think I'd known all along: "I'm not made of money, and neither is my happiness." And I don't need to add to my bank account to invest in my life.

Sweet Charity

Catherine Newman

Please note that I am not a financial adviser. My husband and I have not put away enough money for our two children to go to college. Our income is freelance. Our little Cape house could use a coat of paint. But we once saved enough from our beer-bottle and tax returns to write such a recklessly big check to the global wellness organization Partners in Health that they promptly sent us a handwritten invitation to a black-tie fund-raising gala. Us, with our thrift-store jeans and library books, our camping holidays and baked-potato dinner parties. "Oh, my God," I said to my husband. "They think we're rich!" This struck us as hilarious. Until our daughter, with the uncanny, unapologetic wisdom of her eleven years, said, "Well, we *are* rich.

I mean, compared to most of the world." And that, of course, is the point exactly. Clean water pours from our faucets; nourishing food fills our fridge; the children are vaccinated against catastrophic illnesses. Our wealth abounds. Ideally, at least in those ways, yours does, too.

Which means we get to be philanthropists! Even if you're having a bad year and you can give only five dollars, write the five-dollar check anyway. But first brainstorm a list of what matters most to you. Maybe it's world health. Or wildlife. Or eliminating urban poverty. Education. Politics. Public radio. Talk through the causes, research the related charitable organizations, and decide how you want to invest in the best world you can imagine.

And remember that you can break your own rules. We gave money to our son's teacher, whose Guinean family had been hit hard by Ebola, even though our policy is to donate not to individuals but to organizations that know how to distribute aid in a crisis. But these are the ill parents and siblings of someone we know personally, and we can't help being touched by proximity. We also have a policy not to hand out money on the street, given that every dollar donated to our local food bank provides three meals a day for the needy—a more sensible investment. But then I hand out money on the street. Because people ask for it. Because they are ragged and hungry, or they have a new baby or an old dog, or they open a toothless mouth to call me "darling."

And also because it brings me joy. Oh, make sure your giving brings you joy. It's a contradiction, because circumstances can be so dire—and are: Roughly 1.2 billion people live below the international poverty line of $1.25 a day, and more than 17,000 children under age five die daily of avoidable diseases and malnutrition. To help chip away at that need is to experience your membership in the human community, your own courageous refusal to turn away from tragedy. Ask yourself, "Does my dog need pajamas more than someone needs access to clean water?" Buying *stuff* is the happiness equivalent of dropping your money into a puddle. Giving it away? That's pure sunshine.

Of course, there may come a day when you really want to clad your corgi in flannel, and so you will, and that will be okay. You needn't carve your privilege into a monument to guilt. You aren't Bill Gates. But an immoderately troubled world demands immoderate attention. An act of generosity just short of panic inducing—that's the sweet spot. Stretch toward it. Reach out your hand and open it.

Helpfulness

Gloria Steinem

———◦✥◦———

A few years ago, after visiting Ghana for a conference on sex trafficking, I traveled to Zambia to stay with some friends who live on the Zambezi River. It's a rural place, full of big-game preserves and small villages where daily life is a struggle. When I arrived, villagers were mourning two women who had gone into Lusaka to prostitute themselves to support their families—and disappeared.

On a big tarpaulin laid out in a barren field, I sat with thirty or so village women in a circle. Talking circles are powerful things: They've given birth to countless activist movements, even revolutions. On this occasion, though, I thought our lives would be too different for us to connect. And at first, shyness did prevail. The language barrier made things difficult. But then the women sang a song, and my inability to carry a tune made them laugh. One of the English-speaking friends I was staying with sang "This Little Light of Mine," and others translated its lyrics. And then a woman from the village told a story. With tears in her eyes, she said she was a widow who only now felt safe enough to reveal that her husband had beaten her.

As is often the case, that one truth teller broke the spell. Other women began to talk about their lives. Many of their husbands worked in lodges where tourists came to see wildlife, but the lodges didn't hire women. These families couldn't meet the cost of living or cover what was to the women the most important expense: their children's school fees. Many wives contributed by farming, but as soon as their vegetable crops were near harvesting, elephants would eat them to the ground. And so, with no other option available to them, some women sold their bodies.

The situation seemed hopeless. But when I asked what would help, the answer was surprising: an electrified fence to keep out the elephants.

Back in New York, a few friends helped me raise the money to build one. I received updates from the villagers: Here was a photo of the area the women had cleared, by hand, of rocks and stumps and weeds; there was a photo of the finished product, fresh shoots of maize starting to appear behind it.

When I went back the next year, the women had harvested a bumper crop of maize. They had food for a year, plus extra to sell to pay their children's school fees. Before I spoke to them, if you'd asked me how to stop sex trafficking in this village, never would I have said, "Find a way to keep elephants out of their gardens."

I call this story the parable of the fence, and these are its lessons: Helping begins with listening. Context is everything. People who experience a problem know best how to solve it. Big problems often have small solutions. And, finally, do whatever you can.

I've done what I thought were big things, like testifying before Congress, which actually had no impact at all. And I've done little things I don't even remember doing, like introducing two people, which I would later discover had made an impact lasting decades. That night on the tarp beside the Zambezi, I had no idea what remarkable things would come of our talk. The art of being helpful is behaving as if everything we do matters—because we never know which things might.

Thanks for the Memories

Alice McDermott

———❧———

When her mother, Katie Lynch, née Eames, died in New York City in the late winter of 1919, my mother was only three months old. Her two older sisters continued to live with their widowed father, but since my mother was still an infant, she was taken in by an aunt. Nearly forty years later, that aunt returned to her native Ireland for a visit. That's when the people in her village told the story they had heard about her younger sister's fate: Katie Eames, they said, went to America and danced herself to death.

Among those in the village who had known Katie Eames as a girl, there was a sense of inevitability about the rumor. Apparently, Katie Eames was a bit of a partyer before she left for America at nineteen. A dancer. A late-nighter. My mother knew already that Katie had been a pretty young woman with a round Irish face and a large hat—there was one photo—and now she knew that as a girl her mother had laid the foundation for the story that served as her epitaph.

They had it wrong, of course. Wrong because the girl they remembered was not the woman Katie had become in America: devoted wife, doting mother, one of the city's hardworking poor. The truth of the matter was that Katie Eames, perhaps weakened by childbirth, caught the flu in the winter of 1919 and died at age thirty-one.

The lesson, I suppose, is that none of us has much control over how we will be remembered. Every life is an amalgam, and it is impossible to know what moments, what foibles, what charms will come to define us once we're gone. All we can do is live our lives fully, be authentically ourselves, and trust that the right things about us, the best and most fitting things, will echo in the memories of us that endure.

I have in my possession another photograph, of my own mother as a teenager. In it, she is stretched out on a couch, her shoes thrown off, her head thrown back, a white camellia, like a burst of starlight, in her dark hair. Someone has written on the back: *Mildred, dancing till dawn.*

And I have in my memory all those nights when I, as a teenager, came rolling home at 3:00 or 4:00 A.M., after too much dancing and too much drinking and altogether too much fun, and saw—just over my stern and furious father's shoulder—my mother wink. Or heard her whispered question as I crawled into bed: "Did you have a good time?"

Something of the rumor and the lie, it seems, finds proof in the blood.

We are at the mercy of time, and for all the ways we are remembered, a sea of things will be lost. But how much is contained in what lingers! My grandmother's Irish epitaph finesses tragedy and dispenses with grief and does a lovely two-step over the hard facts of a short life. What remains is that Katie once was a girl who laughed and danced and had some fun. And it's the best, truest thing I know about her.

What Does It All Mean?

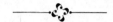

Living is a form of not being sure. . . .
We guess. We may be wrong, but we take leap
after leap in the dark.

—Agnes de Mille

Vision

Kate Braestrup

When he was a little boy, my son Peter spent hours filling sheets of paper with detailed drawings of human conflict. His soldiers carried fearsome weapons. They were borne into battle clinging to the gun turrets of enormous tanks, while flocks of fighter planes wheeled across a Magic Marker sky.

The ordnance in these drawings were neatly labeled in accordance with Peter's understanding of human good and human evil: An American flag fluttered proudly above the good guys, and, in case the point was missed, Peter would write *U.S.* across the flanks of their fighter jets and tanks. The bad guys fought under red flags inscribed with swastikas. Peter labeled their tanks and airplanes, too.

They were the *NOT-SEES*. It was so perfect, I couldn't bring myself to correct his spelling.

Vision as a metaphor for human spiritual insight has a history so broad, deep, and obvious that it doesn't require much elucidation. "I was blind, but now I see" is just one familiar variation on the theme of an opened eye meeting light for the first time.

As a six- or seven-year-old, Peter named evil as a failure of vision. I believe he coined the term "Not-See" not only because the phonetics worked but also because it made sense to him spiritually. The Nazis refused to see the human reality of their victims, and those who might have helped the Jews refused even to bear them witness. The Holocaust began with a denial of human commonality, a rejection of that human "us." This, Peter sensed, is the prerequisite for all violence, all enslavement and bigotry, all genocide, and for all the small and crummy cruelties we human beings busily and blindly inflict on one another.

Mine is a simple spirituality: I am called to love my neighbor. Sometimes, despite an extensive and expensive theological education and few obvious hardships or dangers to distract me, I fail to do this very simple thing. I am brusque with a salesclerk or scowl at another driver in the parking lot, or I might just lose my temper and scream at my beloved son.

Oh, yes, I have screamed at Peter. Why? Well, sometimes because, let's face it, the kid was bad. But mostly it was because I was tired or afraid or pissed off at the world or at myself. I am not so melodramatic as to compare myself with Hitler when remembering these failures (though Peter, now a teen, might do so), but I wince. So it becomes part of my spiritual practice to confess it: Forgive me, God, for I have at times been the Not-See, squinting, blinkered, foolishly resisting the light of love as it stubbornly, by grace, keeps shining.

My Mother's Journals

Terry Tempest Williams

I am fifty-four years old, the age my mother was when she died. This is what I remember: We were lying on her bed beneath a mohair blanket. I was rubbing her back, feeling each vertebra with my fingers as a rung on a ladder. It was January, and the ruthless clamp of cold bore down on the world outside. Yet inside, Mother's tenderness and clarity of mind warmed me. She was dying in the same way she had lived, consciously.

"I am leaving you all my journals," she said, facing the shuttered window as we lay there. "But you must promise me that you will not look at them until after I am gone."

I gave her my word. And then she told me where they were. I hadn't even known my mother kept journals.

A week later, she died. That night the moon looked as

though it were encircled by ice crystals. I told myself it was the illumined face of my mother.

In the disorienting days following her death, I often felt like I was drowning in loneliness. Many weeks passed during which I was simply treading the turbulent waters. I finally sought out the journals as a lifeline that could pull me to solid ground.

They were where she'd said they would be, downstairs in a closet, meticulously aligned on three hidden shelves. Each was bound in cloth—floral prints, denim, linen—their spines more akin to quilts than books.

I ran my fingers across their backs just as I had rubbed my mother's back; in that moment she felt very present. And suddenly the journals seemed too private for a daughter. I realized how little I knew of my mother's inner life, how little of herself she revealed to others. I was afraid of her hidden heart.

I closed the closet. I would wait. Better to leave them for another time, when I might be in greater need.

Upstairs, I made myself a cup of tea. It was a beautiful winter day. Salt Lake City was a mirror of white light reflecting off recent snow. Mother had left me her journals.

It was my birthright to read them. I finished my tea and walked back downstairs. Now was the time.

I opened the closet and pulled out the first journal. It was blank. I flipped through the empty pages. Nothing. I opened the second journal. It, too, was blank. As were the third journal, the fourth, the fifth, the sixth. I went through every journal on every shelf praying to find her script, but all I found was a collection of white pages perfectly bound. My mother had left me her journals, and all her journals were blank. I had hoped to find her deepest thoughts, her dreams, her struggles, alongside her wisdom. What she left me were her silences.

My mother was a beautiful woman with short dark hair, hazel eyes, and high cheekbones; I always thought she looked more French than American. She was the deepest woman I knew and also the most shallow. She devoured Tolstoy and adored *Photoplay*. She traveled to London to hear Winston Churchill speak, and once she deliberately tripped Elizabeth Taylor at Sardi's in the hope of forcing a conversation. (It worked.) She loved my father and loved creating drama. On his fortieth birthday, she wrapped all his presents in black. My mother rarely cried. Autumn made her turn inward. At the end of each day, she walked outside and quietly applauded the sunset.

I was aware of silences in my mother, but nothing had prepared me for the shock of her journals. The blow became a second death. It felt like a terrible cruelty. Like an intentional joke. A message I could not read.

So painful was this moment in my life that I tried to bury it. Almost immediately, without ceremony, I began writing in her journals. I convinced myself if I wrote enough, manically filling each book, the emptiness she bequeathed me would vanish.

It never did. But now, twenty-five years after I first opened the journals, I am finally able to think about what this emptiness means.

To say that she left the journals for me to fill with my own words because she could not find hers is too easy, too simple, and too sad. My mother was more complex than that and far more subtle.

She was also a trickster. She was not above mischief.

The only thing I have done religiously in my life is keep a journal. I have hundreds of them, filled with feathers, flowers, photographs, and words—without locks, open on my shelves. I have journals with field notes from travels to the Arctic and Africa, from days spent at the Prado, from time shared with prairie dogs. Daybooks with calendars, shopping lists, and accounting figures. I cannot think without a pen in hand. If I don't write it down, it doesn't exist.

Mother knew this about me. On more than one occasion, as I was making notes at an art museum or on a hike in the mountains, she'd say, "Look up; you're missing it." She knew how her empty pages would confound, confuse, and haunt me.

Of course, the journals might have been her attempt to follow the promptings of her faith: Mormon women are admonished to write in a journal to record their thoughts, which will become their history. But Mother was a radical soul in a conservative religion. Focusing on the past did not interest her. As a woman diagnosed with breast cancer at thirty-eight, looking back was a luxury she couldn't afford. She didn't have time to waste on herself. She had four children to raise.

And she raised us to expect the unexpected. "Look more closely," she would say. "Listen more carefully. There are secrets in the world." It was Mother who showed us how to write secret messages with lemon juice. She would pick a lemon, roll it on the counter, slice it, and squeeze the juice into a bowl. We would write our words with paintbrushes on parchment paper. A match was lit, the flame burned beneath the paper, and what was hidden magically appeared.

I think about lighting a match beneath my mother's blank pages. Perhaps her journals were written with invisible ink. And it comes to me that her journals were written in code. This I understand, because I have a code of my own. When I want to see deeply into my soul, I will write a sentence by hand and then write another sentence over it, followed by another. An entire paragraph will live in one line and no one else can read it. That is the point. There is an art to writing, and it is not always disclosure. The act itself can be beautiful, revelatory, and private.

If my mother had a mantra it was this: Trust your instincts. My instincts tell me my mother's journals are a mystery. My mother was a mystery. She loved making people think. My mother's journals make me think. And perhaps what looms largest in my mind now, what I could never have known as a woman in my twenties or even thirties, is that my mother left me her journals because she knew they would demand that I listen—carefully—to what is not being said, to what can never be said, only felt.

The journals teach me how nothing is as it appears. An empty page can be full.

If my mother had written the truth of her life, I honestly believe she both felt and feared it would be at someone else's expense. If she wrote about her sons, their father, a family business that separated her from the boys she raised, it would be breaking another code, a code of conduct that says you don't expose your sorrows or your vulnerabilities. If she voiced her doubts about a religion that had all the answers, it would not only hurt other people, it would incriminate her. Better to keep the faith by keeping quiet. Her words could cut, reveal, and wound. And that she could not bear. My mother remained true to her character: graceful, present, and hidden.

Her fears were well-founded. As a writer, I have learned that each time I pick up my pen I betray someone. Some will say I am betraying my mother here. I just have to make certain I don't betray myself.

I, too, fear exposing my truth, standing alone, account-able. But it was my mother's capacity to listen to what I had to say that has given me my voice.

My mother chose me as the recipient of her empty pages and allowed me to fill in the blanks. I will never know what she was trying to tell me by telling me nothing. But I can imagine. If only *she* had known I was her sister instead of her daughter.

Blinded by the Light

Martha Beck

My religion is called Do-Be-Do-Be-Do, pronounced "doo-bee-doo-bee-doh." The final word, "doh," is Japanese for "the Way." Thus, Do-Be-Do-Be-Do could be said to mean "the Way of Do-Be-Do-Be." According to the religion's only member—me—it aims to balance the active "doing" of Western religions with the serene "being" of Eastern religions.

This name is meant to sound silly, because like Reinhold Niebuhr, I believe that "laughter is the beginning of prayer." But when it comes to religion, I can be as serious as typhoid. Born into an intensely religious tradition I would later leave, I've studied and pondered the subject intensely. I've come to believe Marx's dictum "Religion . . . is the opium of the people." Or, at least, part of it. Marx wasn't wrong—but he didn't know that opiates aren't purely negative. They can drug us or poison us or sustain us. In fact, we naturally produce the "endogenous opioids" necessary for happiness. So a quest for truth isn't about being a glazed-over religion addict or cold-turkey atheist. It's about learning which opiates are healthy and testing each new idea before we take it into our systems.

My friend Drew never thought much about spirituality until a college friend took him to hear a charismatic preacher. Drew was immediately hooked. Listening to Preacher X, he remembers feeling "high as a kite. I would have walked on fire, juggled rattlesnakes, done anything the guy said." Drew embarked on a religious journey that now makes him blush. "I'd always questioned authority, but when I met Preacher X, that way of thinking sort of zoned out. I was like an addict: I felt stoned on being part of the group and on thinking we had the Truth. You know, no questions or uncertainty."

Drew dropped out of college and moved into a commune with other followers of Preacher X. "I was euphoric for more than a year," he says. "Then problems started coming up, some from inside my mind, some from outside." Drew found himself questioning Preacher X's insistence that he alone knew the mind of God. Soon after, a seventeen-year-old friend told Drew she and Preacher X were sleeping together. This major buzzkill finally jolted Drew out of his religious "high."

Drew now regrets this whole uncharacteristic episode, but in truth he was following deep-rooted patterns of human behavior. The great sociologist Max Weber hypothesized that every cultural movement began when a charismatic leader gathered a group of followers. The word "charismatic" is important: Though we use it to describe charming or impressive people, "charisma" also means the ability to connect with the divine. People follow charismatics because they purport to speak for God, providing compelling claims that help people feel guided, protected, and united.

This psychological pattern is the reason people attach passionately to value-based groups, from street gangs to political parties. It's why reasonable people may become irrationally loyal to such groups. We're wired to experience euphoria when we belong to a band of people championing common values. It literally intoxicates us.

Compared with the other side effects of religion, getting high off religious participation, even becoming "addicted," as Drew says he was, is a relatively innocuous one. There are greater threats—and not just from Jonestown-style cult craziness. Mainstream religions present their own dangers—because their substantial history, sizeable populations, and organized structure make their members even more certain that they have the Truth. When another group shows up with another version of the Truth, all hell can break loose. Us-versus-them thinking can swell from prejudice to unspeakable violence. The Crusades, the Holocaust, 9/11, and countless other atrocities had religion at their cores. The perpetrators were so stoned on being Absolutely Right that they never noticed the mind-blowing irony of hating in the name of love, killing to defend the commandment "Thou shalt not kill," and waging war under the banner of peace.

One regrettable consequence of this is that onlookers often conclude that religion causes the violence done in its name. Many well-meaning atheists believe that getting rid of religion would eliminate ideological discrimination and violence. Some believe this so strongly that they become angry, even violent, and . . . oh, hello! Here we are, back at holy war! If you doubt that doctrinaire atheism is as dangerous as doctrinaire religion, study the history of communism in the twentieth century. You'll find the same charismatic leaders claiming to know the Truth, the same us-versus-them psychology, the same intoxicated evangelism, the same unfortunate habit of slaughtering people by the millions to improve their lives.

In short, absolutism is the opiate that turns the masses into ideology-addicted murderers, whether religious or irreligious. Doctrinaire atheism keeps the bathwater aspects of religion and forcibly ejects the baby—the one thing religion has that atheism lacks: spirituality.

Remember those natural endogenous opioids produced by healthy bodies—the ones Marx never knew existed? As a depressed teenager, I became addicted to them. I exercised maniacally, triggering surges of feel-good chemicals like endorphins, until my body basically fell apart. I developed a chronic pain condition that left me too crippled to do much besides lie still and breathe. Since it was one of the few things I could actually do, I began meditating. I hated meditation, but only for about ten years. That's how long it took me to realize that this practice could "turn on" the same natural opiates I'd once gotten from exercise. Unlike the rush-and-crash of my physical-fitness addiction, however, meditation seemed to slowly fill a calm reservoir of joy that pervaded my life. I'd become my own source of connection to the divine. Literally and figuratively, I was making my own opiates.

The following is my recipe for Home-Brewed Charisma:

Embrace Uncertainty

The most powerful protection from the inherent dangers of spiritual seeking is to accept that human knowledge can never be absolute. I mean, you could be dreaming right now—of course, you aren't . . . but if you were, how would you know?

René Descartes, one of the fathers of modern science,

dwelled on this question until he felt, by his own description, "dazed." Ultimately, he decided that the only thing he was sure of was that he wasn't sure. Most people know Descartes's famous statement *Cogito, ergo sum* ("I think, therefore I am"). But he actually wrote *Dubito, ergo cogito, ergo sum*. "I doubt, therefore I think, therefore I am." Though we like to ignore it, uncertainty, not certainty, is the philosophical foundation of science.

You'll be vulnerable to "bad drug" religion until you can repeat these words without freaking out: "Nobody's absolutely sure of anything, and that's okay." This frees you to do consciously what most people do unconsciously—make your best subjective judgment about the veracity or fallacy of any truth claim.

Test Every Idea with All Your Senses

The embrace of uncertainty replaces absolutism—the source of ideological toxicity—with a simple, open question: Since no truth claim is absolute, does this make sense?

That was the seditious thought pattern that made my friend Drew question Preacher X's ranting. It's what led Copernicus to dispute the religious "truth" that the Earth was the center of the universe. It's what led the American Founding Fathers away from theocracy and toward democracy.

Asking if something "makes sense" has multiple meanings. It asks us to test a claim with both our common sense and our senses. Modern science owes its incredible advances to focusing on data perceived by our physical bodies. But other advances, like the "self-evident" truth of individual equality, resonate with a subtler, inner sort of knowing. Drew's problems with his cult came from inside and outside his mind because our observations come from obvious physical experiences and intuitive ones.

We frequently reference physical sensations when discussing metaphysical ideas, calling on all five senses to describe something that ostensibly can't be sensed: "I can see how that might be true," we might say. "It sounds right." Or "Something about it feels weird." "I smell a rat." "It leaves a bad taste in my mouth." Some spiritual traditions refer casually to the five subtle senses, in addition to the five physical ones, and suggest we use all of them to decide whether we want to accept an idea into our belief system. That's why I chose, as my own religious hymn, the song "This Smells Funny, and I'm Not Gonna Eat It." If you get a queasy feeling from any of your ten senses, back away. Don't swallow it.

Notice Whether an Idea Unifies or Divides

The word "religion" derives from the Latin *religare*, which means "to bind together." I finally fell in love with meditation when I felt it reconnecting me with my real self, with humanity, nature, the entire universe. This experience of oneness, "at-one-ment," lies at the charismatic core of every religious tradition. So as you go along your spiritual search, observe the long-term effect of every doctrine and practice that comes your way. If it breaks, shatters, or destroys, it's not religion—its absolutism. That drug'll kill you. Real religion, by definition, makes things whole again. It heals.

"The problem for me," Drew says of his youthful

religious experiment, "wasn't that I got high on religion. The problem was that the high was artificial. What I really wanted wasn't groupthink, it was love. Real love— the kind that takes time, testing, solitude, service, stillness, effort, the whole spectrum of religious practice."

In other words, Do-Be-Do-Be.

So it seems Drew and I enjoy the same natural opiates, that we're following the same basic religious path. We sometimes walk together and enjoy the other's company, but we don't need to be in lockstep. We trust our souls to the embrace of uncertainty, to the reliability of our senses, and to the grand, mysterious impulse that has always led human beings to create religion. Imperfect, foolish, and fallible as we are, each of us seems to be designed—and maybe even guided—to find our own Way.

Cooper's Heart

Rebecca Gummere

In human gestation, the precursor of the heart, called the heart tube, forms in a region known as the cardiogenic field. On or around the twenty-third day, tracing the path of some invisible template, the multiplying cells begin a right-looping arc, developing in the form of a spiral, as would a rose or a seashell or a galaxy.

More than forty years ago, Spanish cardiologist Francisco Torrent-Guasp, using his gloved fingers, separated the tissue of a bovine heart at the naturally occurring juncture where the ventricular myocardial band circles around to meet itself. He unfurled the organ, spreading it out flat, a reminder that while for centuries science has continued to treat the heart as a four-chambered construct, there is an added dimension. The heart is also an elegant Gordian knot of one continuous muscle that with each beat contracts and relaxes, pumping blood out and allowing it back in. In the course of one day, the adult heart will beat more than 86,000 times, in one year more than 31 million times. By age seventy, a human heart will have logged upward of 2.3 billion contractions, taking cues from the electrical impulses that move through it like lightning up a staircase.

Even the heart of a baby who lives just forty-two days will pulsate more than 6 million times before its final, fluttering beat.

"Are you ready?" asks the pathologist.

I nod, making a chalice of my hands, and he reaches down into the plastic bucket and lifts my son's heart and lungs out of the water. I feel a slight weight, as if I am holding a kitten or a bird.

I blink and the world turns sideways beneath me.

Cooper was born on a Sunday morning in October 1982. In every way, his arrival was ordinary. He was delivered after eight hours of labor; following his first breath, he let out a sharp, lusty cry, his body turning a healthy pink as oxygen moved through his bloodstream. He scored high marks on the standard Apgar newborn assessment. The pediatrician observed that his six-and-a-half-pound birth weight contrasted with that of our first child, Liam, born weighing nearly nine pounds, but she did not appear concerned and made no further comment.

That evening a report came on about a tropical storm that had hit the coast of Central America. Watching the grainy footage of tearing waves and flailing trees, I felt a wrenching, not of physical origin but something deeper, more terrifying, so that my breath came in short bursts. I turned off the television and pushed away the dinner tray. I was being silly, I told myself. Hormones and exhaustion, I thought.

That night Cooper fell asleep partway through his feeding, his mouth working the air for a brief moment before he sank into the crook of my arm. The nurse said some babies need encouragement and suggested I uncover his feet.

On the second day, after his circumcision, Cooper

stayed in my room and nursed a little and slept, nursed and slept again. The nurse said he was probably worn out from the procedure.

On the morning of the third day, as we packed to go home, our pediatrician stopped by to say she was "hearing a little heart murmur." She suggested we take Cooper to the children's hospital to see her friend, a pediatric cardiologist. She said murmurs are common, that nearly half of all newborns have them. She did not seem overly concerned. "Just to give a listen," she said, signing the discharge papers.

The cardiologist, a trim man who looked to be in his early forties, met us in the hospital lobby. We followed him into the elevator and up two floors to his office, where he performed a brief examination, narrowing his eyes as he listened to our son's heart. Then he draped the stethoscope around his neck and, with a quick smile, told us he'd like to get some X-rays.

We followed him down a hall and into a room where two technicians were waiting. One took Cooper and held him while I removed his clothing, leaving him in his diaper. She placed him on a small saddle with his arms above his head, while a hard plastic case was fastened around his torso, holding him there like the tiny victim of a stickup. He wailed furiously. We watched from a window in the next room as the X-ray machine swiveled around him, capturing images from numerous angles.

After the X-rays, he was taken for an ultrasound. This time my husband and I sat holding hands in the waiting area. It's probably nothing, we assured each other. They're just being cautious, we agreed.

When at last we sat in the cardiologist's office, he placed a chair across from us so that his knees almost touched ours. He held a notepad in one hand, a pen in the other. We moved forward to see what he was drawing, to listen as he deciphered the blue scrawls filling the empty page.

"Do you know what a heart looks like?" he asked, and I remember having one distinct thought: *We should run.*

Outside in the bright October day, traffic hummed along as if everything were normal, as if I were not holding a baby whose blood pressure was at once too high and too low, blood backed up in some vessels like a clogged river, slowing to a trickle in others, whose aorta narrowed to the width of a sewing thread just below the heart, whose lungs were compressed by his enlarged right atrium and ventricle.

Early the next morning, we returned to hand him over again, this time to a lion of a man with massive hands and a mane of graying reddish hair, a pediatric heart surgeon who—while we paced like animals in a crowded waiting room awash in the smells of French fries and cigarette smoke and body odor—would make a long, delicate incision in our son's small torso, beginning just under the sternum and traversing the left side of his body around to the back, removing the scalpel just under the left shoulder blade. He would pull back the flesh and uncover the mistake, cut out the narrowed section, and resect the aorta so blood would flow unimpeded and pressure would stabilize, and the small heart that had been working so hard could ease into a sure and steady rhythm.

Six hours later, the surgeon came to find us. "Everything went fine," he said. I wept into his broad chest.

In the NICU—the neonatal intensive care unit—there was neither night nor day but another kind of time altogether. In a far corner of that too-bright room was a plastic bassinet, and inside lay Cooper, his eyes wide with shock and pain.

Four days later, my husband and I were able to hold him. The next day I was able to nurse him. When we brought him home on the tenth day, he had already gained a pound, and once he was in a regular feeding routine, he was able to sleep. His cheeks grew round, and he kicked his legs in excitement.

I let myself breathe.

On an overcast morning in early December, Cooper, now six weeks old, wakened fretful and vomited after his morning feeding. My husband was away on a business trip, so I dropped off Liam at a friend's and took Cooper to our pediatrician. She gave him a thorough examination, listening intently to his heart, his lungs, his pulse points—all, she said, sounding normal. She thought he had likely picked up a virus and prescribed electrolyte fluids and rest.

Back home he continued to fuss, ate little, and toward evening had a short bout of diarrhea. After Liam was in bed, I called my husband, who was preparing to board his overnight return flight. We chatted about his predawn arrival and the trip he'd been on—anything to avoid naming our fear. Then I sat in the quiet house and listened to the ticking mantel clock and rocked Cooper, and after a time he quieted and was able to take a little fluid, and we both dozed in the chair.

Then this: He wakes, fussing, squirming. I change his diaper and notice he is cool, so cool to the touch, and his skin has gone white, his surgical scar now a harsh purple line against his pale torso.

And then: I am on the phone with the pediatrician, hating to bother her because it is nearly eleven at night, hating to be so inept, but I tell her about this new thing, this coolness, and she says, "Try putting him in a warm bath and see if that doesn't help."

So I do. And it calms us both, but now I cry, too, afraid and very tired, and I talk to him between my fits of weeping, saying, "There. Isn't that nice? Doesn't that feel good? Aren't you better?" He lies in the tub without kicking or moving, looking up at me. I listen to his quiet breathing and watch his dark eyes watching me.

I dry him off and dress him in a pine-green fleece romper and tuck him inside a cotton flannel receiving blanket and then wrap a crocheted afghan around him. I bring him downstairs and rock him some more. Now he sleeps, but I am unsettled. His face feels so cool. I call the pediatrician again.

"Okay," she says, "let's put him back in the hospital till he gets over this," and tells me she will meet us there.

I call my neighbor Jerry to come take Liam to their house. I call my sister-in-law to come with me to the hospital. I put Cooper on the sofa. I notice his lungs sound congested, and this is concerning, this rattling sound is new, but he is resting at last, so I lay him next to a cushion and run upstairs to pull Liam from his bed, and he is sleeping so hard he cannot wake up. His legs buckle; he's just two years old, but I struggle to hold up his deadweight as I try to dress him. I carry him downstairs, where I place him on the shag carpet and slide his arms into his winter jacket, stuff his limp feet into his boots, pull his hat onto his head. He sleeps through it all.

My neighbor arrives. I am saying things like "the baby" and "my sister-in-law" and "the hospital." Everything is whirling.

And then in an instant I feel a terrible pulling inside

me. I let Liam slide to the floor and look across the room at Cooper.

"He is not breathing," I say, and I know it is true.

"What?" Jerry is confused.

"He's not breathing." I run to the sofa, peel away the layers, unzip the fleece, draw up his undershirt. Lay my ear to his cool chest. All I hear is the thud of my own heart. I take a deep breath, lift my head, place it on his chest again.

"Call nine-one-one," I shout, and then everything is changed.

I hold him, panicked, try to breathe into his mouth, try to push on his small chest, but I don't know what I'm doing, so instead I rock him and I whisper because I have no voice. "Please, God, not my baby, not my baby. Please don't take my baby."

The door bangs open. For a moment there is confusion. At first the EMTs go to Liam, asleep on the floor, thinking he is the one in distress.

I cannot speak, hunched over Cooper, trying to breathe for both of us.

"Over here," yells Jerry.

They take Cooper from me, put him on the dining room table, a table I will later have to give away. They listen and look and listen some more, for a long time, with grim faces.

At last one of the paramedics pronounces what we all know: "This baby is deceased."

A sob escapes from one of the squad members, a young dark-haired man, and he wipes his eyes. "I'm so sorry," he says.

My husband arrives home sometime before four in the morning. I meet him at the door. He sees my face and behind me our pastor and the pediatrician and friends and neighbors, and he shakes his head, saying no, and refusing to come inside, putting his hand out and saying no, no, and no. Then his legs give way and he falls to his knees. We kneel together on our front porch, first light creeping from the east.

When the coroner arrives, my husband and I hold our baby and stroke the blanket covering his small, cold body. We kiss his forehead and tell him we love him, and we hand him over one last time.

Since he has died at home, an autopsy is mandatory.

We are devastated to think of him being cut open again, but we have no say in the matter, and we sign the papers, allowing the hospital to do what it must.

Liam sits next to me on the sofa and asks again where the baby has gone, and I tell him again that the baby was very sick, and it was a kind of sick that couldn't get better, but it's not a kind of sick you can catch, you are fine. But the baby was sick and the baby died and now he is in heaven with God. I tell Liam God is taking good care of our baby, but I am not sure I believe it, not sure at all.

I want God to be real. I need there to be Someone in charge, and I need there to be a heaven, someplace where I know my baby is safe and cared for and loved. I think back to when I was a child, moments when I sensed a presence—at eight, seated between my mother and sister in a church pew, the sun painting my legs in reds and golds and blues, believing God was somehow in that dance of color; at twelve, perched on a hillside as a wild wind stirred, then quieted in the field behind me, and then in the utter stillness came the piercing call of one lone bird, sending chills over my skin, the very voice of God in my ear.

Where are You now? I wonder. Friends from a Bible study I've recently joined come to sit with me, read psalms, offer prayers against the descending darkness. *Where are You now?*

Sometimes, late in the afternoon when Liam is napping and the house is quiet, I hear a baby's cries coming as if from some distant room. I startle each time before I remember what my doctor has told me, that these are "phantom cries," common with women who have lost a child.

In time the phantom crying ceases. I clean Cooper's room and box up his clothing, keeping his cotton hospital blanket and a small stuffed bear, and some days I sit in the rocker and hold them close to me.

Six months later, I am pregnant again. My husband and I are terrified at the thought of another loss, and we know this baby will not replace the one who died, and yet there is an urgency toward more life, our arms aching and empty.

When Maggie is born, healthy and lively, I am filled

with joy and fear. I am on my guard so if she starts to slip away, I can snatch her back. This time I will be ready.

I worry Maggie will suffocate while I nurse her. After she finishes, I put her on my chest, where she falls asleep. I stay awake and count every breath until the birds begin to stir and I know we have made it through another night. I worry, too, that Liam will catch something fatal. My stomach aches, and sometimes I feel dizzy and far away. My church friends tell me to trust God. They tell me they are praying for me.

But Maggie doesn't die, and spring comes, and she is robust and round, and when her brother makes her laugh, a tiny dimple appears in her right cheek. Then it is another year and another, and I am forgetting altogether about dusting the pictures of Cooper on the mantel.

By this time, Liam is in kindergarten, and Maggie is in day care. Now also, faint fault lines begin to show in our marriage's foundation; grief is the uninvited third party that has refused to leave.

All the while, I attend my Bible study class. I am on a mission now, poring over the Scriptures, looking for clues, patterns, a key that unlocks the secret door to the place that holds the answers I seek. At the end of the class, I am still searching.

It is early fall when I enter seminary. I am part scholar, part detective, both parts waiting to be struck like Paul on the road to Damascus, knocked facedown in the dust, then renamed, remade, given new eyes to see some revelation of God woven in the very fabric of the universe. I find I'm good at constructing the theological system. There is a certain satisfying logic to the if-then sequences that I'm able to make solid in my academic essays.

I falter, though, when a friend with headaches is diagnosed with an inoperable brain tumor that will take her from her three young children in a couple of years. I lose my footing when a local teen shoots himself one night while sitting on the seminary steps, and we come to class the next day to find his blood puddled on the pavement. I can barely stand to watch the devastation on TV; it seems the world is unraveling at its center.

I learn Hebrew, deciphering from right to left the cryptic

marks on the page, and wait for something to be revealed. I parse Greek sentences, looking for the meaning behind the meaning. I read the Desert Fathers and Mothers, peering through their eyes at ancient sunrises, trying with them to see beyond the far horizon. I study the systematic theologians, listen to their conclusions, weigh and measure them against what I know about babies who slip away in the night.

Always with the same question: *Where are You now?*

Seven years after Cooper's death, I begin the supervised chaplaincy I would need to complete in order to be ordained. In our city there are several possible sites: four hospitals, an addiction treatment center, and two nursing care facilities.

One of the sites is the children's hospital. Many who choose it quit the program before completing it, crushed by the horror of suffering and dying children and their own terrible helplessness in the face of it all. I have driven past this hospital each day on my way to the seminary and never without a stab of sadness, recalling Cooper's tiny form in the bassinet in the corner of the NICU, where the babies were too sick to cry. Since he died, I have been there only once, to visit an ailing niece, and that day I could barely make it through the front doors.

Having counseled me through my ongoing crises of faith, my adviser strongly suggests I cross the site off my list. I know he has good intentions. Still, I feel an overwhelming urge to apply there.

"I can't explain it," I tell him as he shakes his head, "but I feel like a fish being reeled in."

On a blustery day in January, I begin the twenty-week program and am assigned to work with children who have infectious diseases, mostly serious respiratory infections and AIDS. I am placed on the Saturday-night on-call rotation, which means spending most weekends tethered to my pager and the emergency room. During the first weeks, several children die on my watch: A house fire takes a three-year-old boy, an aneurysm kills a four-year-old boy, meningitis ravages the body of a seven-year-old boy, a five-year-old girl riding without a seat belt is catapulted through a car's windshield. I am frequently called up to the NICU.

I lose weight, unable to eat more than a few bites at a time, and become exhausted and frequently ill from sleepless overnight shifts, the days and nights bleeding into one another. While I offer prayers for and consolation to frightened children and shattered parents, my raging conversations with God continue, shared only with my colleagues and supervisor.

As part of our instruction, we gather weekly for training with various hospital staff. Halfway through the program, we are visited by a pathologist, a soft-spoken older man who has come to talk with us about the autopsy procedure. Toward the end of the session, he passes around a photocopy of a sample autopsy form, and at the bottom of the page is a familiar signature. This is the man who performed my son's autopsy.

Later that day I go to the morgue and ask for an appointment. I want to know more; I want to know anything I can know. The pathologist asks me to come back the next day, when he will be better prepared to meet with me.

The following afternoon he shows me into a conference room, sits me at the large table where he has placed

Cooper's full autopsy report, and goes over it, page by page, translating every detail and stopping to answer each of my questions.

When he closes the binder, he turns to me and begins explaining his role in training medical students and his special area of interest, the heart-lung system, describing how he procures and preserves the organs during the autopsy to use them in teaching, injecting them with dye so students can see where problems have occurred and how repairs might be made.

He is quiet for a long moment and then says, "I still have your son's heart and lungs. Do you want to see them?"

Is it odd to be joyful in such a moment? Do you think it unseemly that my own heart leaps, that I feel an indescribable elation, the breath in me suddenly expansive?

In the brightly lit morgue, the pathologist and I draw on latex gloves and move together to a stainless steel sink, where water is running into a white plastic bucket. Reaching down into the bucket, he brings up all that remains of my son, and in the next instant I hold in my hands the heart that had been inside the infant who had been inside of me.

I peer at the small, gray mismatched lungs and examine the stitches on the aorta, stitches that were sewn in nearly twenty-seven hundred days before, while his father and I sat in the waiting room, holding on to each other when we still knew how.

As I cradle my son's organs, the doctor uses one gloved finger to open the dissected heart, showing me the holes in the septum, the wall between the two atria. "Here, and here, and here," he says, pointing, and I stare at each in turn, at the defects that in 1982 had been undetectable in our three-day-old infant, yet powerful enough to kill him.

I stand there for I don't know how long, breathing in the faint odor of formalin, trying to see what I am seeing, so unreal does it seem that I actually stand holding my son's remains.

At some point I begin to do a new thing, to move beyond grief and guilt into wonder, to celebrate what I was part of creating—not what was lost but what was alive, what moved and pulsated deep inside of me, what seems to be in some way part of me still.

After a while I hand my son's organs back to the

pathologist, who lowers them into the bucket, where they float like rare creatures of the sea.

Do I believe God led me there to find Cooper's heart?

Yes.

No.

I don't know.

What is God, anyway? I am no longer certain, if I ever was. Over the years, visited again by loss—of my marriage, parents, dear friends—I stepped past the boundaries that seek to define where God resides and moved beyond ordained service, beyond church, dancing now along the far borders of what might be called faith.

Here is what I can attest to: I went into a hospital basement broken in certain places and returned mended, restored. I went there thinking I knew what I knew, autopsy report in hand, and discovered I knew next to nothing at all, for here my son had been all along, teaching. And here was my answer: There is no answer. But there is love, the kind that binds us to each other in ways beyond our knowing, ways that span distance, melt time, rupture the membrane between the living and the dead.

I like to imagine that we are all of us part of a many-chambered construct love is continually building, its glimmering hallways winding in and around us, and that from time to time an unheard sound comes from another room, noiseless, beyond our comprehension, received as a tug, a whirring in our heads, a flicker in a dream, a vibration along the invisible thread that connects us.

We are troubled, we are stirred, and we are not certain why, but something in us answers.

The Point

Barbara Ehrenreich

The facts are incontestable: We are born, we reproduce, we die. The question is Why? Many decades ago, around the time when I was first becoming aware of other pressing issues, such as skincare and boys, I began to ask that very question.

When most people inquire as to how and why this planet and life of ours came to pass, as most people do, they are offered a one-syllable answer: God. Which is to say, the world is the invention of an invisible, all-powerful being, spinner of galaxies and sculptor of continents. As for what God wants and why he is doing all of this—well, that is a "mystery" far beyond the pay grade of our puny human intelligence. End of story.

As for myself, I never received the God answer. My parents were proud atheists. In the family legend, one of my great-grandmothers, disgusted by what she saw as the church's greed and indifference to blue-collar people like herself, refused last rites, ripped the crucifix off her chest and threw it across the room. We were rationalists who had no dealings with invisible beings, nonbelievers even in the face of death.

The day I gathered my courage and hit my mother with the big Why, she seemed insulted, as if I were questioning the value of her existence—the scrubbing and sewing and cooking. So I resolved to be stealthier about my questions. You can't tell people, "I'm on a mission to discover the purpose of life." Not if you're hoping to prolong the conversation.

I had no notion of what form the answer to my question might take or where it might be found. Would it be in a book I read or in a place I visited? Coded or in plain sight? Would it take years of patient study to comprehend, or would it come in a rush of revelation? And if it was available, why didn't anyone ever find it and mention it? As an adult, I sampled a wide slice of accumulated human knowledge, from physics to theology, looking for clues. I continue to look.

Plenty of times over the years I have been ready to admit defeat, deciding that my mind, for all the expansion it's endured, is simply too small for the task. I try to get used to the idea of dying before I ever find out what I or any of us is doing here. But then there will be a glimmer. A pattern will emerge. The afternoon sun will seem to slant at a fresh angle, revealing familiar objects in a new light. A phrase from a medieval mystic will stir my soul. And each time this happens, I return to the old question: "What does it all mean?"

I still don't know, but I can tell you this: A few years ago, a five-year-old swiveled around to me in her car seat and, totally out of the blue, said, "Grandma, why are we alive?" Ah, I told her, to love and help other people, of course, and—I continued, although I could see that her attention was already drifting—one of the reasons we're alive may in fact be to ponder that question. Because it had just occurred to me that the work of answering the question Why are we here? may itself be part of the answer. Asking after the purpose of life gives our lives purpose.

Contributors

Katie Arnold-Ratliff is *O*'s articles editor and the author of the novel *Bright Before Us*.

Martha Beck, an *O* columnist since 2001, is also a life coach and author. Her books include *Leaving the Saints, Finding Your Own North Star, The Joy Diet, Steering by Starlight, Finding Your Way in a Wild New World,* and, most recently, *Diana, Herself: An Allegory of Awakening.*

Margarita Bertsos has been an editor at *Glamour, Redbook,* and *Dr. Oz The Good Life.* She currently develops content about women's health and well-being.

Kate Braestrup is a community minister, law-enforcement chaplain, and the author of several books, including *Here If You Need Me, Marriage and Other Acts of Charity, Beginner's Grace,* and *Anchor & Flares.*

Bonnie Jo Campbell was a National Book Award finalist and National Book Critics Circle Award finalist for her story collection *American Salvage.* Her other works of fiction include *Mothers, Tell Your Daughters* and the best-selling novel *Once Upon a River.*

Barbara Ehrenreich is the author of seven books, including the *New York Times* bestseller *Nickel and Dimed, Bait and Switch,* and *Living with a Wild God.*

Rebecca Gummere recently completed a nine-month cross-country RV pilgrimage, which she chronicled at chasinglight-ajourney.com. She's currently working on a memoir about the experience.

Thich Nhat Hanh, a global spiritual leader, poet, and peace activist, is the author of numerous books, including *Peace Is Every Step*; *No Death, No Fear*; and *Anger: Wisdom for Cooling the Flames.*

Jessica Ciencin Henriquez is a writer and editor who lives in New York City.

Michelle Herman's books include the novels *Dog* and *Devotion*; the essay collections *Like a Song, The Middle of Everything*, and *Stories We Tell Ourselves*; and a book of advice for children, *A Girl's Guide to Life.*

Marie Howe is the author of four volumes of poetry: *Magdalene, The Kingdom of Ordinary Time, What the Living Do*, and *The Good Thief.* She is also the coeditor of a book of essays, *In the Company of My Solitude: American Writing from the AIDS Pandemic.* Her poems have appeared in *The New Yorker, The Atlantic, Poetry, AGNI, Ploughshares, Harvard Review*, and *Partisan Review*, among others.

Amy Maclin is executive editor at *O.*

Alice McDermott is the critically acclaimed author of eight novels, the latest of which is *The Ninth Hour.* Her novel *Charming Billy* received the National Book Award for fiction. Her novels *That Night, At Weddings and Wakes,* and *After This* were all finalists for the Pulitzer Prize. She is the Richard A. Macksey Professor for Distinguished Teaching in the Humanities at Johns Hopkins University.

David McGlynn's work has appeared in *The New York Times, Men's Health, Real Simple,* and *Parents.* He is the author of the memoir *A Door in the Ocean* and the story collection *The End of the Straight and Narrow.* His memoir about fatherhood will be published in June 2018.

Valerie Monroe is *O*'s former beauty director and the author of the memoir *In the Weather of the Heart.*

Catherine Newman, writer of the blog Ben & Birdy, is the author of the memoirs *Catastrophic Happiness* and *Waiting for Birdy,* the middle-grade novel *One Mixed-Up Night,* and the kids' craft book *Stitch Camp.* She lives in Amherst, Massachusetts.

Julie Orringer is the author of *The Invisible Bridge: A Novel*, and *How to Breathe Underwater*, a short story collection. Her stories have been published in *The Yale Review*, *The Paris Review*, *Ploughshares*, *Zoetrope: All-Story*, *The Washington Post Magazine*, and elsewhere. She is the recipient of two Pushcart Prizes, and her work has appeared in numerous anthologies, including *The Granta Book of the American Short Story*, *The Best American Nonrequired Reading*, and *The Scribner Anthology of American Short Fiction*. She lives in Brooklyn.

Katherine Russell Rich was the author of the memoirs *The Red Devil* and *Dreaming in Hindi*. She died in 2012.

Elissa Schappell is the author of the short story collections *Use Me* and *Blueprints for Building Better Girls*, and is a cofounder and editor-at-large of *Tin House* magazine.

Joan Silber is the author of eight works of fiction, most recently the novel *Improvement*. She lives in New York City and teaches at Sarah Lawrence College.

Gloria Steinem is a writer, lecturer, activist, and organizer, and a cofounder of *Ms.* magazine. She is the author of several books, including, most recently, the travelogue *My Life on the Road.* She lives in New York City.

Ellen Tien is a former staff writer for *The New York Times.* She lives in Manhattan with her husband and son.

April Wilder is the author of the story collection *This Is Not an Accident,* and her short fiction has appeared in several literary journals, including *Zoetrope: All-Story, McSweeney's,* and *Guernica.* She lives in San Diego with her daughter.

Michelle Wildgen's novels include *Bread and Butter, But Not for Long,* and *You're Not You.* She is an executive editor at *Tin House* magazine and the editor of the anthology *Food & Booze: A* Tin House *Literary Feast.* She lives in Madison, Wisconsin.

Terry Tempest Williams, whose writing has been anthologized around the world, is the award-winning author of seventeen books, most recently *The Hour of Land: A Personal Topography of America's National Parks*. Her other titles include the environmental classic *Refuge: An Unnatural History of Family and Place*, as well as *Finding Beauty in a Broken World* and *When Women Were Birds*. She lives in Castle Valley, Utah.

Rita Wilson is an actress and singer who has released two albums, *AM/FM* and *Rita Wilson*.